D1436574

SUFFOLK YESTERDAYS

To Christine Rebecca Jobson
and the
Suffolk Tomorrows

A Frolic at Dunwich, in the Seventies

SUFFOLK
YESTERDAYS

ALLAN JOBSON

HEATH CRANTON LIMITED

First published July 1944

This edition reprinted by Cedric Chivers Ltd., Portway, Bath. 1968
at the request of the London & Home Counties Branch of the Library Association
by arrangement with the copyright holder.
Printed offset lithography by
Redwood Press Limited of Trowbridge, Wiltshire.

CONTENTS

LIST OF ILLUSTRATIONS

THE COUNTY

It is a measuring cast, whether this proverb pertaineth to Essex or this county ; and I believe it belongeth to both, which being inclosed countries into pretty quillets, abound with high stiles, troublesome to be clambered over. But the owners grudge not the pains in climbing them, sensible that such severals redound much to their own advantage.

Suffolk Stiles—Fuller.

If you would transport yourself into old Suffolk you need go no further back than the Nineties of the last century and the early years of this, which is still within the ambit of many now living. Elizabethan fingers still stretched out into those years, in laws and customs ; especially those relating to the poor, of whom Suffolk villages contained many. Traditions handed down the years were the inheritance, to be handed on, as the furnishing of the cottages and the implements of the field. Mechanisation had made but little progress, although the steam engine had done something to herald in the first Great War and the total eclipse of the old order. Even now it is not difficult to find isolated instances of old customs and manners, but these must inevitably die with those who practice them. But would you live again, in truth and reality, the scenes of Morland ; handle in their utility the implements pictured in his interiors, warm your hands at those wide open fires, and " chill " your beer in that warm glow, you need only return, as aforesaid, to the days of grandfather and grandmother of pious, happy memory. God rest their souls, for they could not be rested now !

And not all of good has replaced their ways and times. This generation would not, indeed could not, return on its path, and though we have lost much we have, in turn, gained much. Think of the grinding poverty, cruelty to beast and child alike, of conditions, of prospects.

But think too, of the amazing economy in which life was lived. Nothing wasted, everything alchemised into service from the dandelion and dock leaf to the last scrap of pig, the last ear of wheat. Almost all requirements could be made by shut knife and patient skill. Coverlets, gleaned thankfully from little pieces of cotton or silk, bestowed by a gracious squiress and her daughters, worked with a witchery of stitchery into a whole, for the old four poster and the coffin-like boxes that made up the bedroom on those wide old plancher floors. Cloth rugs, made from an infinitude of pieces, and not without design, for the brick floor, with here and there a "seggen" mat by father in his spare time. Cowslips, currants, rhubarb, sloes, bullaces ; distilled into the loveliest of wine. Milk, and such milk, into butter, such butter ; that salt, deep yellow butter, printed with the wooden prints into the design of a sheaf or a swan, or maybe, a full-uddered cow ; weighed into oblong pounds on those scales with wooden pans. And cheese the less spoken of the better ; but then you can hardly expect butter and cheese out of the same pan of milk !

And how rude some have been about our cheese :—

> Those that made me were uncivil,
> For they made me harder than the devil !
> Knives won't cut me ; fire won't sweat me ;
> Dogs bark at me, but can't eat me !

Here revolved the seasons, aided by scratch dials or clock, of sowings and reapings ; winter and summer ; day and night ; cold and heat. Often they could neither read not write but they could read the sky unerringly ; read the weather, know how to snatch a harvest from the most delusive of skies, for " them spiders, rot 'em, have been rushin' about and filling their webs." The women to brew, bake, sew and churn ; the men to plough, sow, muck, scythe, thatch, hedge, ditch, manage a " hoss " or a bull. Rear cattle and sheep, pigs, and, in their spare time, use their shut knives to make a few platters for the table, for use with those old black-handled knives and two-pronged forks, or their bill hooks to make hurdles and gates, and plait a few rushes into mats for the floor. A fine economy with little or nothing wasted ; goose-down for the beds and segs for the underlay. Segs again for the chair bottoms ; for as the old saying has it : " If it won't pudding, it will froize (fry)."

It is all in the hearts of these men and women ; the men with that far-distant look of the sea in their eyes ; the women in the curious rise and fall of their voices. These people who never bathed themselves from one year's end to another ; and after all why should they ? It was only dirty people who needed to do that ; there wasn't a bathroom in the whole village, or the next, where the squire lived, or the next. But from their old fustian clothes, patched and faded, and the black of the women, with their white aprons, came a fragrance distilled from field and farmyard, pleasant to the nostrils, soothing to the mind.

And making their way along these ways, we and are, the old farm carts, painted in the gay colours of blue and red ; colours which came direct from the ancestors of the Middle Ages, and which happily survive to-day in the wheelwright's shop. Red that fades to a fleshy tint of pink, with great lumbering wheels that smell of grease and grit, and grind like the mills of God over the rutty roads. Tumbrils, waggons, morphadites ; all drawn by those sandy punches with their bare legs ; or perchance a Percheron from just across the water. Emperors, Dukes, Hero or Champion ; Bragg, Diamond, Dapper or Bonny, as they amble along, whisking the flies with their long and ever-restless tails, jingling their brasses, tossing their manes. And you can see the dust flying as they plod across the ten acre, drawing a straight furrow.

And here was work for everyone ; boys and girls, men

and women. The boys to go clappering the crows with their " Ka-ha-hoo." Hold the horse's head in the harvest field and cry loud enough to be heard in the corners of the parish—" Holdyer " as the waggon moved to the next shocks. Bring the cattle home, chop up the beet and ride the best horse. Learn to manage the Goaf horse in the middlestead of the barn, piled high with unstacked corn. A test of horsemanship and endurance for both boy and beast at such an awkward height and with such an uneven keel. The girls to help in the dairy and with the housework, carry " elevenses and fourses " to the harvesters working in the sun. The women, wearing, perhaps, one of those pleasant lilac sun bonnets with the wide curtain that fell on the shoulders. These had a thousand jobs,—attend to the gleaning, collect and wash the eggs, stone picking at a halfpenny a pail ; these later to be turned over to the stone breaker to be chipped and used for the roads, to be worked in by the ponderous wheels of passing traffic. This, of course, was an endless task for as the old farmer said : " The stones, bless yar haart, they grows and as fast as you clean a field on em there's another crop ! " Pea pulling, do the baking once a week, the brewing and, in their spare time, the needlework and manage a brood of children ; airing these latter in one of those ponderous wooden-wheeled perambulators that should have resulted in a fine breed of horse riders, the bumping being good for the liver. For of course large families were the order of the day, " ullus one in t' cradle," and they grew up hugger-mugger in those tiny cottages of our ways, two rooms up and one down. Father, mother and baby in one, " gels " in tother and boys in the cupboard, which was really a small built-in blind room running at the back of the chimney. No problems of morals then, the mingling of the sexes acted as its own prophylactic, and boys and girls grew up to be clean of limb and clean of character. Toilet made out of doors at the pump in all kinds of weather, in those smooth, wooden, square, sloping-sided bowls that got so slimy if you weren't careful, but which resulted in lovely fresh complexions for the girls, and the boys.

The men, of course, did all the other jobs, being the mainstay of the family finances. Starting off at day-break with their wickle pokes full of food, and a bottle of beer to last the day; they " cuppey whay'd," " weeshoed," and brought the " hosses " home just as the sun set between them " grut owd ellems yonder." Carted the muck; there were some fine deep muck-heaps then; repaired the estate with new gates and posts as required; made everything rather than buy it; laid the hedges; cromed out the ditches; ringled the pigs; dipped and sheared the sheep; sat up all night with Bessy the cow; thatched the stacks; threshed the corn; bent their backs to the scythe in a fine rhythm, or dibbled in the seed. Having tanned faces; old and young alike; ear-ringed; smelling of earth and horse; wearing ancient hats that creepled on their heads, an ancient flat dish-like form of felt in winter, straw in summer; the only distinguishable difference in dress to mark heat from cold—necks nearly as horny as the hands. And in his spare time he will see to his garden or bit of allotment; and, speak it softly, a bit of poaching when he ought to be abed !

And what did they live on ? Not a lot of meat, other than salted pork, for Pot days were few, though there were such things as rabbits and chickens; but huge huncheons of bread and cheese, with beer for breakfast, dinner and supper. And maybe a Yarmouth capon (herring). On the old hake over the fire hung the pot with the vegetable stews, into which, for a substantial meal, would be dropped those dollops of dough called spoon-puddings, into the boiling mass; and as a filler up on a Sabbath one of those long puddings, boiled in a " pudden poke," a yard of which helped to make many a Suffolk boy into a man ; and which gave rise to the saying, " Everything has an end, and a pudding has two." Fresh vegetables, freshly cooked, as lovely in their tasting as a fish straight out of the water into the pan.

And we must not forget the letch bucket for making washing Lye, where even the wood ashes were turned to soften the water for the month's wash. The water filtered through the ash into a tub beneath. While many a good brew has been made from the rain water, which many housewives preferred to well or pump for that purpose. But we must not forget also, the candle mould, an indispensable adjunct to any well-run household.

And surely, no garden was complete without its " shod," which contained a litter of all things useful or to be of use. On ancient nails hung the array of ancient implements, some of which latter were riddled with holes denoting time's fretting hand. Scythes, sickles, flash-hooks, bill-hooks, flails, rakes, hoes, dibbers, lines, sieves or riddles, measures, traps, mud-skuppits, a cruden barrow, coarse hempen sacks, skeps, clappers, stools, and whips or whipstawks. All made from hedge-row timber, hand smoothed by constant wear, gleaned with a great eye for purpose and treasured as of great price. And one must not forget the home-made pair of gloves, rough sewn but of great use in dealing with hedges. Here too, were the brewing utensils, keelers ; while hung up in the roof were the herbs and a few bits of seeds that might even yet germinate under sun and weather ! Maybe a pewter candlestick, with a circular base and a tall central stem. One or two horse hames ; certainly an old crumpled horn lantern, coated with grease inside and out, but capable of showing a light on a dark and blowy night. And yes, a bavin fork ; and away in the corner an eel pritch which might be wanted at any time.

But not least of the charm of Suffolk, and our village, was the fact that we had a word for it. A vocabulary, as rich and as fertile in its sufficiency, as the fields, which those who spake it, tended. Even a tree was divided into portions ; the stem was the bole or " right up " ; the large branches, " wrongs " ; the smaller ditto being " chatter bushes " ; but the lower small branches were " washboughs " ; the crooked parts, " crochets " ; the short stunted shoots, " spars " but the new shoot " fifers." Knots were " biests " ; bark, " pill " ; and the toppings off, " stowens " ; but the little bits went to the making of " tit-faggots." And surely there is music hidden there ; the music of the trees.

Then muggy weather was " puggy," or the mist was a " roke," which might lead to " leasty " or wet weather. But a meteorite was a " thunder-pipe " ; and no mean description that !

As for bodily ailments, they were well provided for in the language of the fields ; and, but how could you better describe diarrhœa than a " tharragonimble " ?

The uninitiated might conclude from our vocabulary that we were an aggressive lot, for we have a mort of words for swackings and such like, but they are only used in corrective senses such as, " I'll lace yar jacket for ye, that I woll " ; or " I'll trim yar wisket ! "

And then, of course, we were very superstitious, for we followed the custom of putting a plate of salt on the breast of a corpse. And we believed that hot-cross-buns, if properly made, that is if the whole of the work was carried out on Good Friday morning, would never go mouldy. While in many a home the Good Friday loaf was baked on that day and kept all the year round as a charm against illness.

But then we believed that the Cross was made out of the elder tree, and if you beat a child with an elder stick you'd stop his growth, and that it was very unlucky to burn green elder !

Which all came out of believing that if you killed a harvestman (a long-legged spider) there would be a bad harvest ; or if horse hairs were put in a stream they would turn to eels !

And how many of our children would repeat and regard the rhyme about God Almighty's cock and hen, the robin and the wren ; or the one :—

> If the robin sings in the bush,
> Then the weather will be " coose."
> But if the robin sings on the barn,
> Then the weather will be warm.

And we were unlucky if we didn't have a goose come Michaelmas Day, for if you didn't baste it on that day you would be short of money until come next Michaelmas. Which might account for so many empty purses !

And as for the weather, well, it took its cue from the first three days of March :—

> First comes David,
> Then comes Chad,
> Then comes Winnol
> Blowing like mad !

*　　*　　*　　*

But with all the change there are many things that are changeless. The shape of ricks against the sky. The old granaries perched up on legs under which the carts nestle ; the creepling roofs of barns and outhouses ; or the sweet smell of field and hedgerow. Haymaking, or a haystack, lose no whit of their fragrance, and a field of beans is a rare feast of smell and colour. Hawthorn and honeysuckle have as great a perfume as when the monks plucked them as they passed. They cut down the hedges a good deal to-day, but they still abound with Shepherd's Parsley, lords and ladies, stitchwort and campion. And who could equal a field of Suffolk poppies ? And, thank God ! there's no change in the clearness of the Suffolk air, or the loveliness of its sky ; while the fantastic shapes of Elms still mark the sky-line and the fields, giving a gracious balance to the scene; and the dark clumps that surround the estates and homesteads hold the mystery that is in them.

THE VILLAGE

In every village marked with little spire,
Embowered in trees, and hardly known to fame.

SHENSTONE.

WHICH brings us to our village. It is said that our village is rather insular, but then you must realise that it is part of an insular county. Added to that it is very close to the sea, which may account for something, so that the insularity expresses itself not only in a fine contempt for town-bred people, with an especial reference to " Lunneners," but also for those " turnpike sailors " whose habitat is inland waters ! Then too, there was always a feud 'twixt ourselves and the next village, for we hardly accounted them as civilised, separated from us by that little finger of water that runs onward, its reed-lined way, to the Dutch-made sluice that, twice a day, lets it potter onwards to join the great North Sea. Yet some venturesome explorers would make an annual trip to Trinity Fair at Southwold, with its garish attractions, naphtha lamps, smoke and noise. And there would be tales of cataleptic women, and wild beasts, and an open-air doctor that extracted teeth, painlessly, to the hearty strains of a brass band, and could cure you of your rheumatism. And how folks went to him even on crutches and came away, at the gallop, without them. And ladies in tights. Was not old Dobbler Brown once observed shyly inspecting one of these females ; eyeing her as he would eye the points of his sows, and then shyly looking round to see if anyone had noticed him noticing her ?

But then our village was an entity when they compiled the Domesday Book and recorded the names of some of its most influential people, to wit,—Gilbert the Blond ; Leuric the deacon ; Esmoda " a woman " ; Alveva a

" free woman " ; and names like Toli the sheriff ; Robert Malet, and the ubiquitous and aggressive Bigod ; to wit, Roger of that line. And there were freemen and villeins ; plough teams and rouncies ; cows, hogs, and sheep ; and a church (still there, thank God, and still thatched), and a mill ; and this link with the times of the good Confessor is still preserved in our water-mill farm.

All of which might go some way to explaining who, why and what we are, for the acres are much the same as in the days of the enquiry, though hedgerows and trees have developed in different directions and certainly three acres are worth more than 12 pence to-day ; while a piece, " 9 quarentenes long by 7 broad," should bring in more than seven pence halfpenny " in a gelt." Then, of course, the old originals have gone and names like Barham, Catchpole, Ling, Woods, Stannard, Free, Marjoram, Bloomfield and Hunt have taken their place. While their Christian names, by which they " Throve," give a clue to the times in which they were born,— Eliza, Pharaoh, Alma, Azor, Keziah, Naomi, Noah and the like.

A few extracts from the Overseers' Books from April 1750 to the year of our Lord 1837, may be of interest and serve to show something more of our life and ways,— 1750, Sept. 18th. Paid for cutting 35 loads of

		£	s	d
	Flaggs	£1	9	2
,,	,, Beer		2	0
,,	,, grounding the Flaggs		17	6
,,	,, Carriage	£3	10	0
Paid 24 weeks collection to Widow Dove		£1	4	0
For laying forth Widow Dove			2	0
Coffin for Widow Dove			8	0
Doctor Bloomfield		£2	12	6
Mr. Shipman for two burials			2	0
1751. Widow Newson, a shift			2	6
1753. Sweeping three chimneys			1	0

May 30th, 1753. Agreed with Joseph Gooda and John Lay

B

overseers of the Poor of Middleton, to attend all the poor of the said Parish that are chargeable to them or shall become so for three years from Easter last and find them all necessary physick and surgery to the best of my judgement for £2 12 6 per year and to be allowed Ten shillings and sixpence for every fracture and to have it paid to me or my heirs every Easter as witness my hand,

Wm. Gibson, Witnessed by Jno Preeves,
John Willson.

Fractured fingers and toes to be excepted.

Goody Booth's Winding		5	0
Rev. Mr. Harris for reading the burial and affidavit		1	6
John Hoggard for tolling etc.		3	0
Pair of shoes for Goody Scarlett		3	0
1754. Paid Jno. Preeve in part of his expences for Ann Dove when she had the Small-pox	£2	8	0
1755. Austing Smyth for thatching		2	0
Goody Bruning, making a Shift and Sheet			6
October 1756 to April 1757. Small-pox bill	£7	7	9½
Paid for J. Wright's breeches		3	6
1760. W. Chapman 1½ yds. flannel		1	9
1 Handkerchief		1	0
3½ yds. Cloth		4	0
To loss on Fordley Rectory		5	0
1761. Paid for Goody Stannard		8	0
Laid out for her at Lambert's (shop)	£1	19	0

Further agreement with a doctor for seven years at £4 a year Midwifery, Small-pox and amputations excepted, Doctor John Garner, Yoxford.

Paid a bill for Girl Molster	£3	0	0
1765. Bread and cheese for 7 people that attended H. Clements,		1	1
Expences in getting Clement's married		9	4
More expences on account of Clement's		2	6
To cash Mr. Simonds for marrying Clemance	£1	16	0
1778. Ringers money		10	0
Washing surplices twice			

These accounts are alright tho they are jamble. (!)

1786. On balancing ye book ye town meeting ye book was 5¾d. in debt. Six shillings was then added, which I never received.

1789. Occasion of Mr. Packard's barn being burnt   7 10

1795. Paid Bounty money for Navy man   £10 13 9

1796, feb. 25. 8 sheets of riteing paper for the out town paupers.   0 0 4

Paid for beer to the Clerk and a letter from Norwich. 7d.

August 1799. Paid what was allowed to the Poor whilst they were under the inoculation   £1 3 0

1800. Paid Mr. Tubby for instructing the singers in Psalmody   14 0

1803-4. Carting 12½ Chalders coal   £5 0 0
Lost by the price of coals   1 14 0
Dp. for measuring out coals   3 0
Allowed a soldier's widow apassing   1 0

1806, April 8th. It was agreed at the Parish Meeting for the Overseers for the year ensuing to be allowed one Guinea for a Qtr. for a year.

Expences created by several passengers travelling homeward from their places whereabouts Ponda,* King of Mercia is said to have slew two of the East Angle Kings, A.D. 642 or about that time.   Nil Paid.

1808. Paid for signing the book, although it was not signed   4/-

1810. Paid Leiston Overseer Middleton part of the bill of maintenance of Button's Substitutes (sic) wife and children, (2)   £2 6 8

Paid Turner setting out the bounds between Theberton and Middleton and I. Savage for going for him   3 0

Out all day myself after the same, spent at East Bridge 6d.

Paid the Clerks for examining these accounts, which they never see heard or know anything about   4/-

1812. Warden and Self taken an account of the inhabitants and journey to Yoxford.   10/-

1813. Paid Potter Clark for warrant and examination of Mary Broom and Order   7 0

---

* This should read " Penda," and is evidently some reference, facetious or otherwise, to Bulcamp, an ominous name in those days, as here was the House dreaded by all poor folk.

Paid her going on foot instead of horse and cart   1   6

Beer and biskets   6

8 Journeys to Yoxford, one to Wenhaston on her account   10   6

Paid for a Warrant to take Mary Broom when she returned in opposition to Order of removal   2   0

1815. Tolling the Harvest Bell 20 days by Jno Bedwell 6 8

1816. Margin has this note,—Please to fill in the blanks as large as you please.

1817. To John Parison, sailor, saved his life, with loss of £300. Proper authority to pass   2   0

Another person dreadfully scalt by falling in a copper of Boiling sugar. Collecting for passage to America   6d.

Cart and horse and boy with old Newson's horse and cart. Could not be had in proper time occasioned the boy   4   0

1821. Numbering the people   £1 10   6

1830. Digging grave of suicide by poison, burying at 12 at night.   3   0

13 Jurymen   13   0

1832. R. Cooper bound apprentice to G. Butcher, Wenhaston for 7 years. Cash paid down £5 and the other £5 to be pd. when half his time is expired.

1835. 46½ doz. Sparrows at 3d.   11   4½

Sparrows bill disallowed at audit   £1   2   3¼

Note by auditor,—" These accounts are very unsatisfactory, the County rate has not been paid although it has been charged and the accounts are otherwise deceptive and improper. I disallow the County Rate."

How close we were to the soil is revealed in the official census figures for 1811,—

Inhabited houses 77. Uninhabited 1. Occupied by 121 families. Engaged in Trade 29 persons. Engaged in Agriculture 79. In neither Trade nor agriculture 5. Males 274. Females 290. Total 564. No houses building. Taken by Noah Foulsham and Wm. Free.

In 1821. Inhabited houses Fordley 52. Middleton 26.
          Families   „   81.   „   48.

None building, all inhabited.

In Agriculture, Fordley 55. Cheifly in trade 17. In neither 9.
          Middleton 26.   ,,   18.   ,,   8.

Males Fordley 176. Females 181. Total 357.
    Middleton 109.   ,,   104.   ,,   213, 570.

In Fordley under 5 years males 17. females 27.
Middleton   ,,   21   ,,   12.

In Fordley over 30, males 2 ; females 7. over 90, males 2 ;
females 2. over 100, males 1.

In Middleton, over 80, males 2 ; females 4. over 90,
males nil.

In 1931 the population was 461, a figure which hardly
needs comment, as it speaks for itself.

As a footnote it should be stated that in the parish
account of the statistics the word " under " is used,
when apparently " over " is intended.

And there is music in the names of our fields, as there
is history ; history of the long years before the Reforma-
tion, if not since.   Of the times when men could conjure
a picture into a name and enclose clay and soil into a
living reality.   They speak of times when fields were
sentient beings, clothed with vitality of yea and nay,
and as such are eloquent not only of those who named
them but of those who tended them through the
transient years, and then returned in the cycle of
vitality to those same fields that gave them birth.—
Cottage Field ;   Upper and Lower Kelsale Field ;
Kelsale 8 Acres ; Cartshed Piece ; Barn Meadow ;
Lower Packway Field ; Winding Field ; Old Meadow ;
Sewell's Field ; Rood Field ; Old Barn Field ; Grove
Field ; Broom Field ; Clay Hill ; Orchard Field ;
Dove House Field ; Walnut Tree Field ; Little Plum
Tree Hill ; Great Plum Tree Hill ; Fifteen Acres ; Ford
Field ; Hall Hill ; Sugar Pightle ; First and Second
Charles and Further Charles Fields ; Seven Acres ;
Stonnells ; Corner, also Front Field ; Cobbler's Pit
Field ; and by way of a little joke, Hundred Acres,
applied to a little tiddly bit of one and a half acres

exactly. Which reminds one of that tale about the traveller on his way through Long Stratton who enquired of a native as to its name. "Ah, sir, its name be Stratton but folks call it Long Stratton for shortness ! "

There is nothing very remarkable about our village ; it hasn't even got a squire, so we have to go just over that invisible border for that gentleman. It consists of a street, which runs through a bit of green, lined by tidy, ancient houses, individual in character, as of their builders ; with their yellow plaster outsides and wide overhanging eaves, that shelter the swallows that come annually and bring luck to the house where they build.

Cruck built or post and pan ; yet forming a pleasing harmony, a complete entity. Their thatch or tile roof " creepling " against the sky, nestling into the marshes out of which they spring. They haven't changed much since the Elizabethan revival gave them birth ; here and there, one has gone into decay and disappeared, to be replaced by another belonging to its peculiar day and time. So went the old blacksmith's shack, black with its tar to keep out the weather ; so went the tithe barn with its capacious bays and huge timbers, tie beams and king posts ; first the roof then the walls, until the skeleton, gaunt and cheerless, followed piecemeal to fire or farm equipment ; and tithe was left to the coinage of the realm rather than the gold of the field. And here, on the Green, is the parish Pump. This is, needless to say, not our only pump, but by reason of its position and significance, might be designated by the definite article. Here, suddenly and but yesterday, a storm of considerable violence sprang up, since, by ways unknown, the communal and age-old water supply became private property, and to settle the dispute a new pump had to be provided by the defeated Council. And then came war, and soldiers and lorries and things to our village, and one of those four-wheeled monsters, its driver coming out from the Bell, made short work of that old pump. " Wiped that up good tidily, thet he did, bor ! "

But our Street is the hub of our universe. Here is the church, set on the one bit of ground rise in our marshes, which tells the tale of centuries in its varying windows— no two alike—its thatched roof and the chevron-leaded spire that rises above its old flinted battlemented tower that holds a peal of five bells and many bats. But then our village, which is really two parishes, hence the " cum," held two churches in this one churchyard, side by side, until the human element becoming too pronounced, and one service interfering with another, there was enacted that spoken of in Holy writ, where it says, " one shall be taken and the other left " ; but this time it was so decreed by the worthy Bishop. The site of the vanished is marked by that flourishing linden ; or so it is said. Yet if you need further evidence you may find it in that gravestone of unfamiliar shape. For if you look closely you will find it is in reality an ancient stone that has been cut to make a modern memorial of 1813 ; and turned inwards, you can see the floriated cross that adorned the tomb of an ancient priest. By which hangs a tale, for the 1813 occupant was in his day the parish clerk, and having found this " owd bit o' stone " marked it for his own memorial and in so doing that of the church of which he only knew in story.

The interior of our church is simple. You will look in vain for tombs of the mighty—recumbent knights in armour and great ladies in alabaster—they are not here ; you must look farther afield for these, although at no great distance for all that. Our parish is one of humble folk only, with never a one rising above the middle class. However, it has a singers' gallery and a wheezy organ of the barrel variety that has ground out Te Deums and Magnificats and accompanied " voyces ben small, subtill, thicke, clere, sharpe and shrylle " through and over those neat little inch-square balusters, and the Royal Arms that give it dignity. Then, of course, being insular, we have a special Suffolk font, with woodhouses and lions complete ; not forgetting its faded black inscription,—

> Cryst mote us spede
> And helpe alle at nede.

The bit of ragged coco matting that runs up the one and only aisle, covers up the white flat bricks, and the ancient graves, including a couple of brasses, small and dark, of which it is said that the " female face is best preserved " ; which is perhaps, by way of a parable. And then on goes the matting to the Holy Table—made in Stuart times ; past the poppy-heads of the pews, and the village carpentry of the reading desk and the pulpit. No rood screen, not a vestige, save the doorway to the loft ; but there is an unusual piscina and a sedilia, while at the South door is a Mass clock. But I have not told you of St. Christopher who looks down from the wall with his very fresh face in spite of his years ; of the little Christ that still rests on his shoulders ; of his staff, and of the boat that fades away into the white-wash, out of which the master's magic was retrieved at some grand clean up. A few memento mori, niches, mullions and mouldings, and the tale is told.

And gathered about the old walls, shut in by another old wall of flint and rubble, capped by neat arched bricks, lie the rude forefathers of the hamlet, under those hummocks and lichened memorials or leaning grave boards. And there's a nice little bit of haysel each year, for he who cares to mow and gather, for it's rich soil in this " stent " ! And is it not true that " A ground sweat cures all disorders " ?

Next the church comes the chapel ; and in many respects is of more importance, for we are a strong nonconformist body here. A square-faced building of red brick, flanked by two doors, fronted by a few iron railings, it resembles much the design you would expect to find on a box of bricks. Squared, small panes of glass make up its windows in the front, thus adding to the squareness and underlining the principles here taught. But at the rear, in the wall which frames the preacher, and towards which the congregation fastens its eyes, is an example, in duplicate, of country Gothic, in two windows with lancet heads. A panelled gallery, supported on neat little iron pillars, runs round three sides, which by its overhang, when the lights are lit, gives the place the appearance of the hold of a ship, with its attendant fuggy atmosphere. Another example of country ambition in architecture is found in the battle-mented vestry which has been built on to the main structure on the side presented to the flanking road.

But " my heart," they can " whoolly " sing in this Bethel. One never need be in doubt as to whether a " sarvice " is in progress. You can hear it on the headlands, and down in the " maashes " ; there's no mistaking it ; led at one time by a flute, bass violin and clarionet, later by a wheezy harmonium. Wesley made his people sing, and we follow Wesley hereabouts, especially in the " Old Hundredth " and,—

> No foot of ground do I possess
> No cottage in the wilderness,
> A poor wayfaring man..
> I lodge awhile in tents below,
> And gladly wander to and fro
> Till I my Eden gain.

And if there was any rivalry among the preachers ; if, for instance, you should say that " owd John preached better than Button " ; well, then you would be told that Button could " pray John's head off."

Here, too, the children came to Sunday school to be taught by old, old people with shining faces and warm hearts. To supplement a meagre acquaintance with the three R's, and to sit " right still," or to have their ears boxed, or to be reached after by " a whooly long owd stick."

Discreetly tucked away in the corner, so that the casual visitor can hardly see it, is the Bell, with its thatched roof, timbered ceilings and capacious cellar. Here the ringers come to whet their whistle, not being provided with one of those huge gotches in their sollar that some ringers possess,—

> When I am filled with liquor strong,
> Each man drink once, and then drink long.
> Drink not too much to cloud your knobs,
> Lest you forget to make the bobs.

And here, too, the preachers at the chapel baited their hosses, while they held forth between the hymns. Here you could often hear the raucous refrain,—

> Sing old rose, and burn the bellows,
> Drink and drive dull care away !

On that little bit of a slope that ends with the church-yard gate is our one and only shop ; founded, built up and maintained by Joseph Broom. Here, from a pack-man's bundle, has grown a marvellous store of all things which a countryman can need, and here is a social centre that rivals even the pub. You can often pick up a bit of news here that might have escaped your acute country ears, for you never knew who you might meet when you unsnecked the door and twanged the bell. Saturday night found a rare clack a going on, that bull's eyes and bacca failed to stem. And sure enough you could find a cap for the boy Jonah, and a pair of mittens for the girl Susie ; to say nothing of one of the grey powders for grandfather. And, as Joe would say,— " You will catch more flies with a spoonful of honey, than with a gallon of vinegar ! "

The old rectory which stands beside where the old tithe barn stood is now let off as a two-dweller ; a new rectory, time of the Georges, having been built amid the trees lower down the road. A nice little bit of square-ness, this latter, with its garden all carefully laid out by an early and wealthy rector, with a magnolia-grandi-flora before its neatly pillared porticoed doorway. Copper beeches and firs, and the glass lean-to that runs along the south side full of flowers, make up a satisfying whole. The kitchen garden, not forgetting the straw-berry bed, is at the rear, separated from our meandering river by the stables and the trees. Damp? Oh no, for it just escapes the attentions of the pernickety river, when that gets a bit overbearing like, and overflows from the old Ford even as far as the Parson's meadow, and makes one go a good couple of miles further round to do the journey dry shod and allow one's horse to keep its feet.

Back-road Hill is probably an old cattle track that comes directly from the Ford just mentioned ; straight from the ancient port of our bit of coast, that was once so famous, at least so thought King John, with its " toppe shippes and wend melles." It goes on past the church, straight over the Street, to the " Carnser," or causeway, built up across the marshes, and on to Bury St. Edmunds. But before you get there, the track leads straight through a corn field, to the other side of our village, to wit the " Moor." Here is a second edition, sans church, sans chapel, sans pub, of our bourg. Here, bisected by roads, that go to and from the toll gate, is a close-cropped green stretch, not so level as it looks, for it drops into hollows that now and again fill with water. Here the gypsies have come, time out of mind, to pitch their umbrella tents, light their fires, leave their distinguishing marks and then pass on to another night. Here have been open-air Baptisms, Test Acts permitting, and here, the great prize fight took place when one man's bare knuckles battered his opponent to death.

And still the sun goes down behind those distant elms, or lights the silver willows that fringe the farmyard pond, glancing on its way across the gables of Elizabethan brick that go to make the farm house, its chimneys and its dial-less niche, and its fragrant old garden. Somehow, one feels to be on top of the world here. A sleeping, smiling world, flanked on the east by a sea; a capricious, grey, uncertain sea ; while to the south the great city and wars and rumours ; too far away to know or trouble. There a mill, and there a tree ; grotesque, human, friendly ; and over all the sky, a Suffolk sky with its winds and its stars ! Backwards, you can just see the thin delicate spire of the old church, rising out of the grey green in which it is set, while the sound of those bells is sweet here, winter or summer, as the sound rises across the sky, torn hither and thither between the stars. Whether the moon hesitates to come out of the water, or the Great Bear to disengage itself from the corner of the old barn, matters not. Here is England of all the years, since the Saxons left their abiding marks of blue eyes and fair hair, and strange wrappings round of words that cross from mouth to mouth, even to this day.

And then, of course, there was our old mill, vanished now, as already mentioned and as so many others. Its old sails twizzled for many a year, and its mass of woodwork purred as the wind turned the wheels. Akin to the sister ships of the sea, its huge massive post strutted up on four brick piers that helped to make the round house, above which the fabric hung. And there amid the ropes and funnels and spars and huge revolving wheels with apple teeth, and wide-boarded floor and wooden dusty stairs, you could get a fine view of the countryside ; and just through that gap yonder a glimpse of the sea, with, perchance, a sail going by. Here came the local wheat, corn, oats, rye, to return to local stomachs via the old brick ovens, the pride of every home. And here, too, came the gleaning ; flour for the hutch, grist for the pig. But it was from our mills that we had our sayings,—

" The miller's boy said so ! " an alias for a matter of common report ; and the other which is a synonym for a piece of one's mind,—" I gave it him, as it come from mill ! "

But we must not forget one great institution in our village, the blacksmith, who housed himself in those black tumble-down sheds, already noted, that extended the Back-road Hill to the Street. Here you could hear, from early morn to after candle light, the music of the anvil, and see the sparkle of the fire. From open doors, littered on the bit of green, were all kinds of parts of things made of wood and iron. Portions of wagons ; wheels, shafts, whipple trees ; portions of ploughs, and even of mills, for the blacksmith could turn his hand to many things, not merely shoeing but repairing anything in the metal line even to the gymmers off the old cup-board, the fastenings of a door, the handle of the pump, or the pendulum of your clock. He could do a bit of wheelwrighting too, and in any case he could keep all the farm implements going, besides providing the furniture for the estate in the shape of gate hangings and fastenings. Scythes, flashing hooks, bill hooks, sickles, anything with an edge ; wheel rims, tie rods, spikes and teeth, or a peculiar bracket for the peculiar break in a piece of old furniture. Nothing amiss, even to the turnspit and its mechanism, or a set of railings with neat little knob heads to be set in wooden cross bars to hem in someone's garden, later to be hidden by climbing nasturtiums or a bush of lavender.

Just opposite to the blacksmith was another village institution in the person of Sam Selfe, the snob or cobbler, who worked in his shed, in the garden of the corner house, as you turn to go across the Carnser. The tappings of his flat-headed hammer, as he hardened out the leather on his lap stone,-were as familiarly musical as his neighbour of fire and anvil. A bit grimy, perhaps, but then it was grimy work, dealing with those " owd butes," and something of the toil of such a trade was evidenced in his frequent bursts of coughing. Yet, like all village crafts, it had a strongly individual aspect which was expressed in the fact that he knew the peculiarity of every son of the village as portrayed in his feet. Not least attractive in Sam, as far as the children were concerned, was his extraordinary ability to swallow whole mouthfuls of rivets and tingles ; how hungry he must have been ; what a wonderful inside he must have possessed ! And what a genius at making wax threads, finished off at the ends with a bristling bristle, that acted as a supple, yet powerful, needle in threading through the leather ; to say nothing of that peculiar tearing, smacking sound as he released his hands from the threads in pulling the stitches together. And when not on boots he could turn his attention to a bit of harness making or repairing, which was to him a kindred business ; while his old tub of dark water mirrored the cobbler and his bench in its tanned surface. Besides, he was a good deal of a philosopher, probably due to the reflective nature of his craft, and often would the more thinking of the village worthies creep into his workshop for a bit of a mardle, including the old mad chemist who had retired to the village. He would come to discuss his religious difficulties with Sam, for he was firmly of the opinion that he was damned one minute though saved the next. Sam's councils went a long way to restoring the peace of his mind.

And after all, the trees are by far the tallest things in our square mile, almost taller than the brass cock on our spire. All the houses are humble, not rising even with their chimney stacks to that of the church ridge. The "popples" down by "Rackfur" ; the Yew just skirting the squire's park ; the Beech with their smooth dappled boles on Parson's meadow. The elms in the churchyard ; and the holly everywhere. The willows that lean athwart the ditches and hold the mists at evening about their tops, making themselves into fairy temples ; or the restless, ever-shivering aspens that fringe the ponds of farmyard and field and make a leafy lament to water and sky. And always the oak, which provided timber for the church, the barns and the little houses ; straight grained, silently powerful, always restless as the old carpenters knew. These all add their distinguishing features to the scheme, so that you would know if one were cut down or fell in one of " them grut owd blusters o' wind." Houses, cottages, farms, barns, outhouses and stacks, creeple into the shape of a bit of rising ground or the misty hollows.

Then too, our parish is not without its distinguishing features of a long and superstitious past ; created from the very people who eked out an existence from wind and weather. Mother Lumkin's hole, where a tumbrel and two horses were lured to destruction. Sarah Cobbler's pit,—and we have a score of pits, mysterious and dark, with generations of neglect, from whence came the sand and what few flints could be found to build the local homes—but only one Sarah Cobbler's. The other are merely pits or holls, of no account except that they bite into fields, provide a cover for the game birds and a bit of scenery to the locality, with a bit of kindling for the fire of the thrifty. And then the Round House, set at the crossings of the way ; ghost ridden, avoided, until parson Packard, with book and key, laid it by the heels and " shet it up in the cupboard set askew in the chimney."

But we had a school in our village, long before the Church built one near the old vicarage, as befitted one next the village where lived the man who was head of the " Society for the Repeal of the Taxes on Know-ledge." Run by dame Gathercole ; the children gathered in her kitchen to be taught the rudiments of reading, writing and sums, and so be a step in advance of father and mother who knew nothing of these things yet managed uncommonly well with their ignorance. All for the large sum of one penny per week, which fee, however, suddenly doubled itself when they began to write. One wonders if there was any go-slow movement amongst the scholars, aided and abetted by the parents, or whether the additional burden was gladly and willingly shouldered. Here the girls learnt to curtsey and sew ; the boys to be respectful, and find their way about with pen and book. Always with their ears cocked to hear the familiar wheeze and whirl of the old clock in the next room as it struck twelve. And if so be that Mrs. Gathercole was just that little bit deaf, then up would go a hand to remind her of the tolling— " Thet hev strook, Maarm " ; and home they would burst as shot from gun. Yet, the course was not of long duration ; necessity and that ever present urge— work, tore them away all too soon to be doing " suffen " useful and add a few coppers to the small store that helped to wear out father's home-made purse with its leather strings.

But our parish is quiet and peaceful. You can lie abed at night and hear the barking of old Noller's dog away on the Moor. " Thet were a worriting about suffen " ; a tramp, a Spirit on the upward flight—for dogs know, where bees have to be " told." An old cow in the " midder " ; the whinny of a colt ; or the wheels of old Bailey's trap, and the clop of his pony's feet, on his way to or from someone in trouble ; grating musically along the gritty road, lights bobbing between the trees. Then owls, but you'd hev tew have whooly fine harin' tew hear the bats ! The squeak of a stoat, the scream of a rabbit. And what's ailing Susan Candler's cockrells, they're whooly making fules o' thesseles ? And they do say you can hear old Susan's hacking cough, down by the Yew tree. Or the time when old Chambers dropped his money out of his trousers pocket when he was going to bed. Joe Broom declared he heard 1/8

Middleton Street

Home of " Weeping Prophet," Rackford Farm

Middleton Green ; Chapel on right

Manor House

fall, and when they asked him how he made that out, he said he counted twenty bangs and he knew right well as how they were coppers because Chambers wouldn't have had anything else. But that may be all exaggeration !

And the roads and lanes thread their way, making a course to the Turnpike, like streamlets feeding a river. Bending acutely, dark with overhanging trees, or sunlit and wind swept. Drifts and sandy lanes, down by Eastlands or up by Title. With every way its house or homesteads, mostly designated by the occupation of many years,—Sperry Free's; Jim Bolton's; Nan Hunt's; Uncle Frank's, or Cousin John's. Here and there an old House Leek could be seen growing on the thatch of the superstitious to act as a lightning conductor. Then we have our farms,—The Dove House, Valley Farm, Water Mill, Rackford, The Hawthorns, and the long two-storied house with square-paned windows, that runs beside the road, and always such a neatness of curtains and gardens. Around the square-headed door are grouped the living rooms. While at the other end, completing the façade, is the dairy, where are white shelves and a stone floor, and those flat round pans, and the fleeters, the stools and the churns, and the ever-lasting smell of milk. Here come the boys and girls from across the fields, with their bright cone-shaped cans with their arching handles ; and the neat clean little baskets with their hinged covers, for the eggs and butter. And the one latticed window, shuttered with the neatest of laths, about which grows the attendant elder to keep off the flies and the witches ; for here is kept the food and the beer.

But this is not all, for there remains the garden house, well named ; for here all the land about is a garden, full of flowers, heavy with scent, bees and birds. And the summer lingers long here into autumn, and the autumn into the shortest of winters, with the spring jostling for

c

place. Another flat-fronted little bit of brick where the
plums and pears thread a way between the windows.
Here too, is a nut grove, built on both banks of a stream-
let, over which the branches and the kernels intermingle,
throwing a deep verduous shade into the sluggard trickle.
Strawberries, sweet peas, cabbages and love-in-a-mist,
mingle with carrots and pansies, lavender and stock.
Yes, it is a Garden house and somehow there are always
chains on one's feet in the passing ; and never were
fetters more welcome.

Although in many respects our village was an outpost
of civilisation, yet we were in touch with the great world,
and that, not so much by the railway which ran some
five miles away, the passing trains of which over the old
pile bridge could be heard when the wind was favourable—
—" that being a rain wind "—but by the sea, which
was even nearer than the railway but in the opposite
direction. Many of the younger men of the village were
fishermen cum-dealers cum-farm workers, who would
be off at various seasons " Herren driftin'," or cod or
ling fishing. Their forbears had gone off in the Iceland
fleets of Elizabeth's days ; dangerous work that, not
merely by the cockle-shell crafts in which the " viage "
was made, but by reason of the Norwegian, Danish or
Dutch pirates that infested the waters ; danger that
could only be adequately dealt with by " waftage " or
convoying by the Royal Navy. Our long ancestry is,
or was, seen even in our longshore boats, the Beach-
Yawls that plied along our bit of coast, amid the seas
that get up so quickly. The great length as compared
with the beam, the grace and strength of the hull and
the sharp stern all point to a Viking ancestry, and
origin !

Our nearest bit of beach was once a flourishing and
populous port, now swallowed up in the great water ;
its only memorial being an old church in ruins on the
sandy cliff and a monastic ruin, surrounded by a

mediaeval wall, with two magnificent gateways flanking the grass-verged road that leads down to the bit of lane that leads to the beach. Here, on the one memorable day of the year, the whole village would go on pleasure bent, conducted thither in farm wagons, decorated for the occasion, hauled by the broad quarters of the local punches ; sweating, whisking their long tails in a vain attempt to keep off the flies.

But this bit of beach was memorable to us by reason of a certain coal trade that flourished here in the spring and summer days. Billy Boy Ketches or Jackass Schooners making the trip, to and from northern ports, laden with coal, would almost beach themselves here and then be unloaded by means of a wonderful old gantry, mounted on two immense wheels that was run out into the water to the side of the vessels. Tumbrils could be backed on to the landing stage, thus made, and the coal unloaded into them. These would then make a tour of the surrounding villages and townships, and the coal be sold in large wicker baskets full by the " chalder " to provide firing for the winter. From the same sea too, we get our fish, fresh and flavoursome, a welcome variation from salt pork and eternal hollow meat (rabbit).

And as we could hear the railway on calm days and nights, so too, in the fateful days of the New Year, we could hear the wild droning of the sea's rage as the North-easter drove a scouring tide along the beach. Then too, at intervals, too frequent intervals, news would filter through of shipwrecks on the Barnard Sands or off the Cache cliff, and a mother in our village would be a son the less and the sea gain a victim the more.

And so the tour of our village is completed. As you stand on the old Rackford Bridge, foot passengers only crossing the creaking planks, hosses and carts go through the stream. For here. from the time of civilisation's first morning, drovers and cattle, friars, packmen and pilgrims have wended their way into this irregular parallelogram which makes our parish. Away to the Pack-way and the Yew tree to the south-east ; right, along the Back-road to the Moor to the S.W. ; back to Fen Street to the North and the ever-restless sea to the east. A compact, self-contained, individual people ; a worthy microcosm of the macrocosm which was England !

OUR NEIGHBOURS

Ill fares the land, to hastening ills a prey,
Where wealth accumulates, and men decay :
Princes and lords may flourish, or may fade ;
A breath can make them, as a breath has made ;
But a bold peasantry, their country's pride,
When once destroyed, can never be supplied.

A time there was, ere England's griefs began,
When every rood of ground maintain'd its man :
For him light labour spread her wholesome store,
Just gave what life requir'd, but gave no more ;
His best companions, innocence and health,
And his best riches, ignorance of wealth.

The Deserted Village—OLIVER GOLDSMITH.

I THINK, perhaps, I should introduce you to our neighbours
in case you don't happen to know them, and for this
purpose we will draw a circle with Middleton as its
centre. But then, of course, it is only a three-quarter
circle, for we are so close to the sea, and to such the
circle can never be complete. It remains true that we
are insular and self-contained, but even so, one has to
do with neighbours if it is only for market purposes.
And then there is always someone who has a relative
over the border—at Pear Tree Farm—or other such
address, which necessitates coming and going at certain
seasons of the year. Perhaps it would be as well then
if we begin in the S.E. corner, which brings us to
Theberton.

Theberton is of importance to us because there lives
the Squire who has the most right to be designated our
Squire. It is a pretty village, containing two or three
parks, and a really fine old church with one of those
round towers for which Suffolk is famous. Of course
you may have heard that Suffolk folk once thought these
round towers were the casings of wells left from the
Flood ; which, when the waters subsided, the soft soil

37

subsided also, hence the Towers. But that is on a par with the clue in a recent cross-word puzzle which ran as follows,—" But are the people backward in this county? " The solution of which was—" Suffolk." Well ! Well ! Need one say more ? It smacks of that story from Charles II about Wooley. Charles said he was a very honest man but a very great blockhead, and that he had given him a living in Suffolk swarming with nonconformists. Nothing daunted, as soon as he was established, Wooley went from house to house, and in time got them all to church, and as a reward for his diligence the King made him Bishop of Clonfert. But what Wooley could have said to the villagers of Suffolk, Charles could not imagine, unless it was that his nonsense suited their nonsense !

But there is every sign that the Round Tower at Theberton is of Saxon origin, and was in all probability first used as some sort of refuge, probably against Danish or Norwegian invaders.

And Theberton has lately, and more recently, another notoriety, for here, in one of its own fields, settled ablaze, a Zeppelin in the first Great War, and the bodies of the airmen lie in its little graveyard, under that inspired quotation,—" Who art thou that judgest another man's servant ? To his own Lord he standeth or falleth." Which suggests that feelings ran high, as well they might.

And under the magnificent lime tree, eastwards of the church, amid its very roots, is a " pulk " of water ; and if you have never seen a " pulk " before, well you can see it even to this day !

They do say, and not without foundation, that the old smugglers hid a good load of stuff under the very altar of Theberton Church ; but I can assure you it is not there to-day !

Eastward of Theberton is East-Bridge, a sort of out-post of civilisation, hanging on, as it were, by a hair's

breadth, lest it fall into the salt marshes and the sea.
A collection of red-brick, red-roofed houses, and a pub
which delights in the name of the " Eel's Foot."   Of
course that house knew more of the smugglers than
ever Theberton Church, for the river which runs along
on the last lap of its journey under a saddle-backed
bridge, passes through East-Bridge.

Further south, beyond Theberton, is Leiston, famous
at one time for its Abbey, the ruins of which still stand
amid the cornfields and the poppies.   And if your eyes
are keen, as you pass along the Turnpike, you can still
detect an artificial mound on which, it is said, they
placed a piece of ordnance with which to subdue the
Abbot and his monks.   This was not the original site
of the Abbey, which was, long years ago, when the
Abbot had wreck of the sea " in the Town of Thorp,
viz., from the Port of Menesmere unto Almouth," much
nearer the coast line ;   but it was moved here for
safety and for its final destruction.   Needless to say,
the Abbot and Monks had far more than wreck and
lagan, for they held the livings of many of the churches
hereabouts, including the two in our village.

But Leiston has a far greater claim to greatness, in
these latter days, in that here, founded long after the
Abbey, is an engineering works that sprang out of an
edge-tool maker, who made the finest edge tools for many
a mile when he started at Wickham Market.   Here too,
sprang up some of the earliest of agricultural machinery,
of drills and such like, shades of Tull, for they were ever
abreast, if not slightly in front of the times.   And
speak it to the eternal honour of this old founder-edge-
tool-maker, that out of him came also the first woman
doctor and mayor !

South of Leiston, is Aldboro, which speaks for itself,
with a Moot Hall, not merely in the Elizabethan manner,
but of and by those days ;   the aforesaid first woman
mayor ;   the birthplace of Crabbe and of late years the

residence of millionaires ! A famous life-boat station and a gastronomic notoriety centreing round the Sprat. Here, too, you will find a peculiarity of river which seems, like the Dunwich river of yesterday, to have had the intention of making union with the sea, but changed its mind, and flows on and on, " and silently beside the sea," separated by but a narrow spit, until it joins force at Shingle Street. If you cross this deep and dark little current you arrive at Orford, but on the Aldboro side the bank is known as Slaughden Quay, and here, in the days when everyone was not in such a hurry, you might have taken sail to Fenning's Wharf or Custom House or Wool Quays, London, in the " Amity," " Plough," " Endeavour," " Resolution," " Alert," " Commerce " or " The Alde," under Captains Dance, Parker, Birch or Green.

Orford, not satisfied with having one of the finest examples of the Norman Castle Keep in its midst, must needs catch a Merman in one of its fishermen's nets. He was a decided curiosity as ancient prints show, " hairy in the hairy parts, except the crown of the head which was bald " ; and great was the effort of the local inhabitants to make him civilised and ordinary in his habits, in the way of wearing clothes and going to church. But it was all to no purpose, he would persist in eating raw flesh and fish, although he maintained the laudable habit of lying down on his couch at sunset and rising at sun-rising ! And so, in the process of time he escaped to the sea and great was his delight as he plunged in and swam away, to be seen no more by mortal eyes for ever. M. R. James in his book on Suffolk and Norfolk, tersely remarks,—" The authority is Ralph of Coggleshall," who was a specialist in this kind of thing, for did he not discover the " fair girl and boy " at Woolpit ? These appeared human in form except that their skins were greenish, and they wore green clothes and refused all food but beans. They spoke a foreign tongue but afterwards, having learnt the English language, they told of coming from St. Martin's Land, where it was always twilight, the people all had green skins, but were Christians. And it was the sound of our bells that lured them through the dark caverns to find themselves here and no way of return. It is said the boy died but the girl lived to wed a man from King's Lynn.

Returning inland, and to the S.W. of Leiston, we come to Cold Fair Green, so named from a Fair that was held here in the cold season of the year. This is a curious collection of shacks and hutments; dumps of old iron and allotments. It is said that the Vikings here made their tombs, and whether this curious Eastern-like encampment is a result of those grave builders, descendants of the hovels in which they dwelt and housed their tools whilst disposing of funerary boats and deceased chieftains, cannot readily be determined. The stacks of old iron are probably some tribute to Vulcan, who is held much in esteem hereabouts, although others would aver they are but disfiguring evidence of the old Lancashire slogan,—" Where there's muck there's money ! "

Beyond Cold Fair lies Friston, noted for three things— Church, Mill, Chapel. The mill purring and " twizzling " to this very day; a lovely sight; all honour to the family who have so gallantly preserved and persevered through all the years. The chapel, a curiously shaped structure, pentagonal, something akin to a Knight's Templar Church rendered in Nonconformity. It belongs to the Baptist persuasion, which may explain its shape by an attempt at grouping round a central bath in which the rite of Immersion is practised. To be seen at its best, one should visit it at Whit-tide.

Fetching our compass round, we come to Saxmundham, a place of importance to us all, for here is the local market. Here, too, are shops, and here lived and throve a maker of those long-cased clocks, without which no one of our homes was complete—to wit John Bright. To say nothing of the old inns, coaching, posting and otherwise—and now our important railway junction.

Further south is Wickham Market, which as its name implies is a rival to Saxmundham in the sale of cattle, poultry, butter, cheese, and eggs. Its tall-spired church stands sentinel on its hill, and contains a fine specimen of a Sanctus Bell in the ridge of its roof. And here, over the doorway of one of its little houses, Hissey, when driving through in his phaeton, noticed the charmingly worded sign,—" Horse Gentler ! "

And sweeping further over lies Framlingham, a lovely old-world place of 18th-century houses, and those more ancient, and shops ; and a church which holds some of the richest tombs and dust in all Suffolk,—the Mowbrays and Howards, not forgetting that Earl of Surrey, the poet. Here are monuments, exquisite in beauty, that remind one of the epitaph on the tomb of Tallis,—" Wherefore he lyves let death do what he can." We must not overlook, too, a very fine "pair of organs" that once belonged to Pembroke College, Cambridge, which have led the singing down the years.

But this, of course, is not all, for here is Framlingham Castle, from which Bloody Mary set out to claim England. And we must not forget good Sir Robert Hitcham and his almshouses, or Thomas Milles, wheelwright, and his contribution to the alleviation of poverty, of which it is said the " wheelwrights Almshouses as far exceeds the Knight's in magnificence, as the Knight's exceeded the wheelwright's in quality."

But while in the neighbourhood of Framlingham we must not miss Dennington, one of the most gloriously furnished churches in Suffolk, almost a rival to Fressing-field over to the North-West. Here are intricately carved bench ends, including that little gem of a Sciapus

—the race of men who used their web-like feet as a sun shade ; a three-decker pulpit, a sand tray, chests, as old as the wood-workers' art, one of the earliest form of ladders, and the Bardolph chapel, with those ancient alabaster figures, enclosed as they are by parclose screens complete with lofts. Here's a place to linger in, with its timbered roof and its perfect riot of wood-work generally.

Whilst on the subject, we might speak of Fressingfield, not forgetting poor old Sancroft, with its bleached oak bench ends and roof to match. If you would see what a sculptor in wood can do, then here it is. Passion Bench, Dedication Bench, and a few dozen saints complete in more than a wooden translation, chiselled to life and loveliness. Here, too, is an old Guild House on the edge of the churchyard, now an inn.

But we anticipate the throw of our arc, and must next to Yoxford, known as the " Garden of Suffolk." Here lived, by means of a little book and stationer's shop, James Bird the poet, he who wrote on Dunwich,— *A Tale of the Splendid City*—and others. Here, too, was an excellent Farmers' Club.

A little West of Yoxford is Sibton, with memories and a memorial in the ruins of its Cistercian Abbey, the one and only of that order in the county. Surely it is fitting that here, on the edge of the Garden village, these monkish gardeners established themselves, and we should not now grudge them the livings they held hereabouts. For it is said that the seed beds which to-day burn in the sun about Coggeshall and Kelvedon were introduced by the Cistercians ! Perchance it was they who caused Yoxford to be called the Garden !

And so the compass swings, taking into its arc Bram-field with its ancient church and its separated Round Tower—be it well-casing or refuge. But inside the church is the gem of those who seek the perfect example of Rood Screen. Not to mention a kneeling knight and his lady, or she who was to have taken herself another husband, but who was " stopt " in the very act, dying of apoplexy.

Of the Knight we might do well to quote the boy's description, as told by Hissey,—" He went to the wars ; she thought him dead ; she fretted herself to death ; he was not killed, but returned home to find his wife and baby (that she had given birth to in his absence) dead : he died of grief two years afterwards." Who the " he " was the boy did not know. " We ullas calls him ' he '." And as you leave the church, notice the " crinkle-crankle " wall opposite, that runs round the Queen Anne Bramfield Hall ! And then on to Halesworth.

" Oh, you'll be all right at Halesworth, it's a town lighted with gas ! " which was surely a great tribute to a place set amid oil lamps or no lamps at all. Here is another fine church, where they have long rejoiced in a society of Bell Ringers. Here you will find the earliest MS. of Change Ringing, dated 1621, stuck in the flyleaf of an old book, and here is the account rendered to the Churchwardens of Halesworth by John Bryant,—

For account of ringing for Lord Nelson's victory of Trafalgar, 3.30, November 7th, 1805.

And here, on July 19th, 1539,—

William Walpole, to the priest, clerk and ringers, to provide them bread and drink, a piece of land, called Bell Pightle.

And here, you could have bought a set of Suffolk Chairs, and even seen them being made, by Thomas Collett or his son George, in his workshop set in one of the yards off the Thorofare. Not the type made by Daniel Day or his son Richard ; they were at Mendlesham, and a creation peculiar to themselves, delicately beautiful. But these at Halesworth were of the common village-home type, and now have a charm hard to equal, with their smooth wooden seats, little spindle backs holding two or three wooden balls. Their mellow golden colour is of the ash or elm from which they were made.

When Hissey came here in the eighties, there was a great Ram's horn charged with snuff, on the hall table at the Angel, and a set of verses, written, it was averred, by the local schoolmaster, set over the summer house in the garden of this same inn, moralising on the game of bowls. Rather than quote the verses, I would retell the soliloquy of the local inhabitant,—

" You be a copying them verses, I see, sir ; they be much admired, that they be. I never read no poetry I like better, that I never did. He must have been a great scholard who wrote them, that he must. The lots of people as I've seen a copying those lines, to be sure ! You see, sir, I ain't had no grand schooling, there weren't no school boards in my time, but I can read, and I knows what I likes. . . ."

" Supposes you baint a poet, bee's you, sir ? . . . Ah, sir, it takes a clever man to write poetry, that it do."

But we must on and take Blyford in our stride, with memories of Bulcamp, once the scene of the earliest East Anglian battles, where Anna and his son Jurmin were slain as recently as 654 A.D. ; crossing the happy Blythe, leaving Wenhaston with its Doom behind us. We pass the hated, dreaded House of Industry, which for all poor folk hereabouts eclipsed any other history of Bulcamp in its wretched significance. Do you wonder there was a riot here in 1765 and again in 1836, and the local labourers, armed cap-à-pie, sought to tear down its walls ? And so to Blythburgh with its cathedral-like church that rises sheer out of the marshes, amid the few clustering cottages. Here is more woodwork, with bench ends holding mutilated versions of the deadly sins, and a roof where angels still hover in spite of Cromwell's shot guns !

And it is but a jump to Dunwich and the sea, which brings us due north of our village, in as complete a circle as a village near the coast can accomplish. But of course Dunwich needs a volume to itself. The only evidence of its former glory, left by the tide, are two gateways, set in an ancient wall that runs round the ruins of its Franciscan Priory. A great gate and a little gate, symbolising the two extremes of society of which England was then composed. And here is the ivy-covered house where lived Edwin Edwards, and where old Fitz came to visit him, seeking the comfort and peace of Dunwich listening to the robin singing in the ivy tods of the old wall. Walking along with, perchance, bare feet, carrying his boots in his hand, and nodding his head "as did all the Fitzgeralds!" Here then, with poppies blowing on the cliffs and golden samphire growing on the beach, and somewhere, in secret, the Dunwich Rose, we end our endeavour to show you what sort and kind of people we are who live in these parts of old Suffolk of this England!

THE WEEPING PROPHET AND SUSSANAH

But good old Baucis with Philemon, match'd
In youthful years, now struck with equal age,
Made poorness pleasant in their cottage thatch'd,
And weight of want with patience did assuage.

    *   *   *   *

Because we liv'd and lov'd so long together,
Let's not behold the funerals of either ;
May one hour end us both ! may I not see
This my wife buried, nor wife bury me !

THEY lived in one end of the farmhouse, now turned
into a two-dweller, on the left fork of the road as you
come in by the old track over the Ford at Rackford.
The road that leads a winding way to the Yew Tree.
John Barham, known locally as the Weeping Prophet,
and Sussanah his wife. 'Twixt these two was a great
contrast, one of those peculiar balances which Nature
often provides.

Sussanah was a tallish, upright woman, frail and
inclined to delicacy. Recessed blue eyes, that gave
her trouble in windy weather, going bloodshot and
rheumy in their sockets. Long thin hands, scored and
hard by the heavy work, with a mass of blue twisting
veins making a pattern up to and over the prominent
" leaders " and knuckles. Reticent and quiet, she had
but little to do with neighbours and made few friends,
but a strong and penetrative sense of humour sustained
her lonely and quiet life. Dressed in the traditional
black, turning green, of her days, with her attendant
bonnet, her thin face and frame took on an almost
pathetic appearance.

Left much alone, she seemed to spend much time
in waiting—waiting for the return of John from some
meeting or other, or from work. Waiting for bed—
waiting for the wind to drop ; for the wind terrified

her. Waiting for the Sabbath—waiting for the barm to work the dough, set in the great red pan before the fire with its covering of cloth.

A refined, gentle creature who found the rough life hard to live, and her somewhat wild husband difficult to manage ; yet she bravely lived from day to day, snatching a bit of humour in a quiet way out of the hardness that was life. His love and admiration for her was as intense as his character ; more marked, perhaps, after she had slipped away to join her little son, than when she sat by a lonely fireside awaiting his return.

But her waiting turned her to thinking rather than to inanity and later to writing—writing to her " gals " away in " sarvice," of the little trivial things that made up her quiet life. Painting with her funny little steel pen, pictures of home and Suffolk. One or two of her brothers left our village, on fortune bent, to found a lucrative and extensive business in the new artificial fertilisers. To become mayors and doctors and " nubbady knows what." But they never forgot the village or their nativity !

John, on the other hand, was one of two brothers living in the village, amongst a very numerous collection of relatives, representing a large family that had sprung up out of a tumble-down shack—even then falling into oblivion—as you get nearer the Yew Tree. This was in all probability an old yeoman family that had succumbed to the years and circumstances. These two brothers—again a study in contrasts—the one choleric, excitable, dogmatic ; impatient of " duzzy fules," who would wave his arms about like a windmill—or as Sussanah to her daughters—" Oh, how he do throw his arms about when he is talking." The other, quiet, reflective, taciturn, but a considerable politician. John and Harry ; but it was the fiery John who was the preacher. Harry contented himself with being " hoss-

How We Lived ; a Double-dweller

Uncle Frank seeing them off

Packway Farm

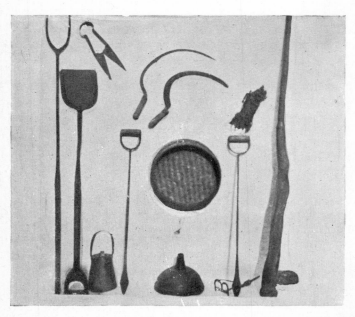

Suffolk Relics found in an Outhouse. Reading from left—an oven fork and shouldered peel, milk can, and above, sheep-shearers; a pair of dibbling irons, and between, a brewing sieve of fine cane, and a brewing funnel. Branding iron and a rammer cut from the hedge. The bundle is a measuring chain with brass tabs

man " and the pleasant company of his wife, leaving apocalypses to his brother.

John had been a farm labourer from his youth up. First clappering the crows, then doing all the thousand jobs expected of a boy—a country boy in particular. He was a skilled member of a highly skilled trade, and much in demand as a thatcher, which was his specialised branch of the industry. By hard work and constant, he came to be the bailiff of the farm, and thus to a little more opulence and responsibility in life ; but the years between had been hard and straitened.

John and Sussanah had launched a family upon the world of whom any might be proud ; a valiant contribution to their age and calling ; and this on some ten or twelve shillings a week, surely an object lesson in thrift. One wonders how it was done, until one realises that there was little or no rent to pay, a good deal of garden, a pig, and, maybe a bit of poaching. No niggard ; for he who is careful provides himself with the means of being generous ; John was considerate to all and especially generous to the Cause. Yet he managed to leave behind a reputable sum to be divided between his children.

Not large, perhaps, as families went in those days, yet too large for them to remain at home a moment longer than was necessary. They must be off to " arn their keep " ; and one by one, as they had come, so they went ; first to local employment and then to that city of dreams and disillusions—London.

They lived in a typical home of the times and our village ; unspoiled, unpretentious. An effortless collection of the antique, the simple, and in its entirety, the beautiful. As this home was typical of the rest of the village, and for miles surrounding, perhaps you would like to recall the picture, for it was before the era of the machine or the cult of the antique.

Tiles had replaced the thatch, and out of the roof crept one or two dormer windows. The front door opened

D

into a narrow little passage, that led straight to the "backus," with a door on the right into the comfortable room. The fragrance of the garden ; which was surrounded by an old flint wall ; with its box borders and sweet-smelling phlox and lavender, penetrated the house and mixed itself with the coco matting, the glistening white curtains and the clothes, the stored apples and the home-brewed ale.

In the front room a fine model of a wing chair—also commode—resplendent in a loose cover of turkey twill, served as the one comfortable piece. Six Suffolk chairs, of a lovely mellow hue and dainty shape, stood about the long-leaved table ; a grandfather clock, bearing a local name, ticked weightily the hours ; a barometer, banjo shape, bearing a tiny convex mirror that brought all the room into its shining compass. A chest of drawers, most useful of articles even downstairs, but then, of course, in this case it simply will not go up ; an oblong framed mirror with half-round columns with gilded necks, flanked on both sides with silhouettes of not too distant ancestors, and one or two religious prints touched into life by flaming mediaeval colours. Two cases of stuffed birds—one an " old harnser," the other a wild duck—shot on the local marshes and evidence of the owner's prowess with the gun that hung from the two hooks in the beamed ceiling. It should be remarked that the case containing the harnser stood on a fine specimen of an old coffin stool, so called, but really the earliest form of seat. On the mantel shelf, the inevitable brass candlesticks, a pair of cream jugs in the shape of cows being milked by wooden-looking milk-maids ; a lustre jug, and Mr. Wesley preaching from under a gothic arch, with the most significant of clocks painted in gilt below—the hands pointing to twelve-twenty-five, and he still preaching and likely to go on !

But we must not forget the brass warming pan, and

the corner cupboard, that just misses the ceiling, with its finely shaped shelves inside, painted green, and hidden by two rather ugly doors. But what a wealth of fragrance when the doors were opened ; of spice, nutmegs and mace ; sugar and currants ; the aroma of tea and home-made wines, which pervaded the room, speaking of age, mellowness and hospitality. And the bureau, with its treasures and secret drawers.

In the " backus " are some rush-bottomed chairs, with shaped flat-ladder slats in their backs, that have travelled since the days when Anne was queen ; an old " mingin hutch " in which is stored the meal for the pigs. While in the larder, as large as a room, are the. brewing utensils and the peelers for baking.

Upstairs, is the also inevitable four-poster, with its fluted pillars, and its heavy faded red rep curtains ; another old chest, reminiscent of a square coffin ; more rush-bottom chairs ; an American clock with cathedral-like face and the loudest of ticks ; and a steel candlestick holding a box of the largest and most fragrant of matches. A few old mats, home-made from pieces of cloth, and a patchwork quilt of the finest needlestitch, provides a coverlet for the bed and the old chest, and completes the room.

The ceilings upstairs were heavily covered with white-wash, while those below were beamed. Flowery, though faded, wall papers, gave a cheery aspect to the old and irregular walls, rounding off the crevices made by the upright, rough-hewn beams and eccentricities of ancient builders. Flat smooth yellow bricks paved the ground floor, with wide, uneven planks for the upper ; and lattice windows, with broad flat sills, let in the sun and kept out the rain. The stairs, steep and evil, rising with difficulty by the chimney as guide, ended abruptly into the bedroom, with the shakiest and smoothest of hand rails across the top to keep one from toppling into the tiny abyss.

This, then, was the home in which they lived, and it was not without influence on their characters, each its own way.

John was no mean preacher for there was a deal of the natural orator about him. Unlettered, but with a strong strain of common sense running through his make-up and coming out in his " sarmons." He could deliver himself of a discourse on the Old or New Testament, with vivid realism, whilst his dramatisation of the entrance into heaven almost rivalled Bunyan for effect and richness, or Blake for imagery. Added to this ability, however, was the inability to control his feelings, with the result that tears streamed down his honest rubicund face, into the beard that fringed his chin ; and his bandana was all too small. Hence his name !

But there was another side to chapel going and preaching, which we are apt to overlook, but of which his wife was very conscious and which creeps out in the letters,—

I am shut up here from one week to another and father is going somewhere nearly every night. I tell him he forget I am alone. If I went to chapel and left him alone I should not stop to the after meeting after the sermon. Then he get riled and say he can't give satisfaction at home nor abroad, so I say as little as possible. I know it would be a thousand times worse if he was shacking about like some ; but still I am alone.

How woman-like that last little return to the fray.

But if the children had gone they were not forgotten, and those pithy little letters written by mother—father was no hand at writing—followed them. Letters written on odd scraps of paper, curiously spelt, cross written and recrossed, until with the greatest difficulty they were deciphered. But they were of home and conjured up a picture as by the hand of the greatest domestic artist.

I am now trying to write a few lines to you as I dare say you think it time I should. Well, my dear, I don't forget you none the less. By the day of the month we were packing you off last year, or will be, the day before Brother's birthday.

This last is a reference to a younger member of the family who survived not, and went, ere his time, to the churchyard. And here is another delightful little reflection of the child,—

I do hope the eggs will come all safe, without breaking. I have done my best about them. I ordered some butter but it did not come so I have sent you what I had as I dare say it will come to-morrow, Saturday, so don't mind my cutting it as I could best get it in the bottom of the tin. I have put two eggs in, I think they have two yolks. Take care of the old tin as I have had it a long time. Don't you laugh now at what I say, but I used to keep Alan's marbles in that.

Father was a not unworthy member of the village band, which made music on all kinds of strange instruments ; not forgetting the " sarpent " and the Wellington bugle ; on various occasions during the year, with an especial reference to Christmas. What a delight it was to hear the strains across the still night air ; and it was still then ; and how much of emphasis could they not put into,—" Christians awake, salute the happy morn ! " Now down in the village street, now by the Dove farm, or up the Pack-way, or across the ten-acre, or away in the marshes. Their breath condensing, fingers freezing but their hearts glowing, and one or two becoming merry by reason of sundry unlockings and the resulting drop of " suzzles." And horn lanterns would lead them home, with the water frost on their whiskers, at " Bull's Noon ! "

Yet strange to say, the band was not always appreciated, as witness the little incident, again recorded in the letters,—

When the bazaar was at Yoxford the band from here was to have gone one evening. Well, no one let father know

nor no one seemed to know exactly ; father seemed like a
nesting hen, as I told him. Well, he waited here till nearly
seven o'clock, then he took his horn and said he would go as
far as Joe Broom's ; well, Joe was then getting his horse
ready to go. Button was at Rouse's corner, so the two carts
started and off they went. As they were playing on the
meadow, out come the man and wanted to know who was
bandmaster ; so Godward said he was. " Who ordered you
here ? " says the man. In short, well, he said he was master
and ordered them off, so they all packed up and came home ;
so was home half-past nine. I persuaded him all I could not
to go. I was rather amused at it although I did not say
so to father.

One enterprising additional source of revenue was the
growing of seed and selling it to neighbours, or at a
nearby township. This entailed a tremendous amount
of work, much of which fell on the woman of the house,
and is duly passed on in the shape of news from home.

I am housed up, cant see into the road who goes past,
with the turnip seed. I tell father it is sickening to have
seed every year as he do grow it. Well, you don't know what
to get or to grow nowadays.
We have been busy after keeping the birds off the turnip
seed ; they get in them trees at the parson's, they are a
trouble.
Oh, how hot to-day, and as I have a few minutes I thought
I must write a few lines to you as I haven't had a chance to
write in day time, as the seed have to be seen to every chance
I can spare. I could not bake last week on that account.
Father put beet down both sides, carrots and turnips in the
middle, which is nearly half the 'lotment. And later,—I am
glad that's done, a lot of trouble but it pay better than anything else. Sold nearly all and got the money.

As the letters throw so much light on both father and
mother, and the little world of home, here are some more
extracts,—

I made a little white-currant wine, a gallon. Well just
before father came in I looked at it and thought I would

taste if it was sweet and all right. Well I set it in a pot. Well behold as I pulled it out of the pot, out come the wine, the bottom was out of the bottle. Wasn't it a good thing I put it in the pot? Never had it served me so before, as I had put it in that bottle a lot of times before. Well, soon got over that for I soon put it in another.

* * *

They are making us a new shed, not so big as the other, not quite. Then father put the onions in the granary time he was away, so I had to pick them over and measure them by the peck, 6 or 7 or 8 pecks altogether, so that took time ; then the taters I have had to help get up so they are all off the 'lotment, all done by littles.

* * *

My feet are so tender I dont hardly know how to hobble about for the roads are so ruff and dusty now. Good-bye for the present, father's love and mine.

* * *

My eyes begin to be dimified so must say goodnight. Father is gone to settle up for the quarter day ; expecting home any minute. God bless you.

* *

Dont know if I shall bake as my flour is dark and old, have had it a long time, got a comb of wheat so had it ground. The peas are not up to much yet, only a few fletchets, want rain so bad if it please God to send it. Father had to go to Halesworth with the sheep wool . . . Friday is Dad's birthday.

I thought I would brew as the weather was so nice, then it would be done for a time, so Wednesday I got my copper ready to fill to scald my vessels. Things get so damp and mouldy, so I had to be so careful that the beer didn't taste amiss, so father filled the copper and I set to and got it hot and scalt them all. Father was out every evening all last week to the Thursday morning, I got up and got the copper to boil, so I managed and done it once more thank God. I am so glad I had the strength given me to do it as it is rather cold, so that got over if| it comes very cold for two months or perhaps three, but I am very stiff from lifting but I hope I shall soon get over that. You will think I have put this letter together very funny to a young lady, but haven't seen so much of city life as you have. What I meant by father being out, is hardly ever at home do he is off to bed in good time. I thought I could have had more of his help when I brewed but, no, on the 'lotment noon time and night, picking out more carrots for seed, so many each time, so I have done them by going a little a time, while plenty haven't done a stroke on either side. He helped me all he could but sometimes some one came, so he could not come fast as I wanted him. I expect I have got 4 or 5 bushels of potatoes on our rooms, wish I could send a bushel up. I often think of you, if wishes was horses then beggars might ride.

*   *   *

I dont think I ever heard of so many being ill before, with colds and influenza as there have been, not about this part every place, and such a lot of deaths as well. Poor Turner Tupper with his heart, mustn't be left nor stoop to do his boots up, cant dress hisself, poor man, he say he is good for nothing . . He was a nice man, Turner, I always liked him, I suppose he can give orders as they are in business.

*   *   *

Father say he wish you was coming but it is the going away makes us feel queer as we grow older every time, all of us. I have had three bottles of medicine and shall send for another. NO, thank you, the pills you left father took and they give him a doing too, only two at a time ; one is enough for me, thank you all the same. Made father a cup of tea at four as have been close by. They have cut one field of wheat down, now are down the drift in one of them big fields.

*   *   *

I feel tired, mostly do from baking, make me so hot then sinking ; it is nearly five o'clock. My places all want papering, upstairs, passage, can't do them alone.

*   *   *

You asked if we had any plums this year, no, about six on that tree you got so many off four years ago. The other one you can't expect as it was moved last year, nor yet the bullisses, but rather more apples on the old tree though not many. I sold a peck and a half of black-currants, give the postman three pints for bringing my medicine, and gave Walters some.

I expect I had drawing on for a bushel with what I gave and boiled down and made a bottle of wine, so done well I am sure.

*   *   *

I should have wrote before, but who should come yesterday afternoon but Aunt Ling, perhaps she may come oftener now she have started off, but did not stay only a few hours as it soon get dark. I shew your likeness to her. She say, what's that the mor Beccky? You know her homely way. Dont see but what she is the same as ever, not so strong but in ways real old East-Bridge, never be anything else now.

*   *   *

Saturday after they (visitors) left I done my room up and swept their bedroom, laid the carrot seed on and done several things and Sunday morning it rained a little so did not go out till evening, when I went to chapel. Then Monday I washed a few things out. Father went on the Moor to thatch after dinner, so I packed his fourses up, so had the afternoon to myself. Cut the onion seed off, soaked his shirt and one sheet, got the eggs up and washed them.

*   *   *

The wind make me feel timid, I am such a strange creature, I get worse the older I get, so nervous. I have had several bullices on the old tree, I go in the holl and pick them up, then I wish I could send you some, but they are rotten ripe.

*   *   *

Thank God I feel better, think I should feel more so, but the weather being so severe just now it makes it bad for everything, so I get up a few hours every day as I am warmer by the fire than in bed, for the sheets feel like ice to your face, then I can manage to keep the fire up for poor father. We go to bed about eight and it is so bad for the stock to feed as well. My eyes are so moderate when I first get up for the first two or three hours. Uncle Harry is better, he took some rum.

*   *   *

Alldridge came home with father one Friday night and stopped perhaps half an hour and told father Charlie Rous owe them £5, and Jethro the same, and that Catchpole by the schoolroom owe him a lot for years. They are both in the class with him, and don't you think it is gall to the man to meet such, and them to stalk up on the rostrum with his bass fiddle and seem as they do.

* * *

Took the old carpets up, washed the old chamber, so it will be a little fresher, cant do much. The stamps are a secret, don't say when you rite in letter. I must do it, I feel better, when I see so many things you have given me, especially if it is the last I have it must go, you would not have a mother in father, he don't think as I do in many things now.

* * *

They are busy after haying, so must make some beer. We can get the granary ready for some of you, but you must hog in and out as you like. Now must go and get the old mare her tea.

* * *

So a load of your old father's furniture is gone. Yes, dear, it wont be as it once was. I dare say you can draw the old place, and father with the old beer mug, yes, so can I.

* * *

The weather hold very dry, it begin to be talked of being serious. Well, we have been a murmuring set as a nation, so it seem as if God is going to punish us by a drought.

* * *

The wind at the chapel is that cruel. I dont go very often and I dont know that it matter much.

* * *

You can believe it or not, but the Prophet really came to London, not so much to see the Queen as one of his daughters. Such an event was a landmark in life, causing, as it did, a marked and significant impulse to his education. After all, how could life be the same again after seeing the Crystal Palace, the Houses of Parliament and " harin' them wonnerful prachers? The folks gooin' ower Lunnon Bridge ud whooly stamm yer ! I fared tew hev my breath took clean away." Besides his stay was not without incident as far as the " gals " were concerned, for they nearly lost him once or twice, especially when the sound of a brass band fell on his ears and he set off in pursuit.

Oh, the preparation; what would he have done without his wife? The talking it over, the excitement, so acute that it ended in a bilious attack that delayed the journey; and, needless to say, it was the subject of many letters.

I dare say you are looking forward at father's arrival in the city. Well he have finished thatching, but not exactly finished, as he go by the week. The others have done as they take it for so much. Hope father will finish up this week, all being well. We have got the onions off the 'lotment, harvesting them, so I hope to get them under cover, and have got the seed beet as well, so that wont take any harm. The carrot seed I can get by littles, so father will stamp it out and put it in a sack. So if he comes up next week, what is on 'lotment wont take any harm till he come back.

And the 'lotment didn't take any harm, and he duly returned to look with other eyes on the little " owd picture o' them Houses of Parliament " that graced his front room. He " reckoned as how he'd been some lucky " when he picked it up at the sale over Peasenhall way. He " ullus did like it and its bit o' colour." But he confided in Sussanah, that he wouldn't like the job of thatching St. Paul's Cathedral,—" no he 'udn't, that he 'udn't ; but my haart thet ud whooly shine in the sun ! "

As you will have gathered from the letters, John was a rare practitioner at thatching,—it was in his blood. No one could rival him at stack thatching, or for that matter, repairing the cottage and barn roofs when necessary. Equipped with his thick kneeling pads, and his split willows, he would soon have " them yelms " in place and the broaches knocked home with his handy home-made biddle. While to watch him " hull " the water over the straw, you might have been deluded into thinking that anyone could do that ;

until you realised there was a knack in it, a twist of the wrist that sent the water shimmering into a pattern over all those straws. While Charlie " Goddard " was a dab hand at making " them little owd straw dollies," which finished off a job of craftsmanship in a craftsmanly manner.

Harvesting was no picnic in those days ; but it was the make-weight of the year, with enough money to pay the rent and a few other debts come Michaelmas— old Michaelmas, October 11th. And one could never have done it without the old " yaller " gotch of home-brewed, kept safely in the shade, to wash down the " levenses " and the " bever " or " fourses." To be followed by " throshing " which would occupy the whole winter, even by the light of the old horn lanterns, and one could hear the rhythmic thud of the " Frail," in the middlestead of the huge barns. They used to say in Essex you could tell by the sound how they were paid,— " By the day ; by the day," slowly, dully ; " We took it ; we took it," brisk and bustling !

> Thump after thump resounds the constant flail,
> That seems to swing uncertain, and yet falls
> Full on the destined ear.

Father is very tired come bed-time, from 4 or 5 in the morning till 7 at night. If the weather is fine, uncle and them will finish this week, not father as he go by the week, and must do the stacks up and cover them. No accidents, thank God, but it have been hot for them all, and us as well, but not so hot for these few days, nor yet nights ; we are glad, aren't you ?

If a preacher, the Prophet was also in demand as a public speaker, providing no mean feature in an evening's programme. Some of the excursions as deputation on dark winter nights were not without incident, as on the occasion when John was persuaded to go to Wenhaston as chief spokesman for the evening.

Two were going from Middleton, to show friendliness and bear with them the quality of novelty as coming from a distance; nine miles to be exact. One as chairman, the other as supporter and old friend. It should be said in passing, that this chairman was not without character, with his tanned face, gold ear-rings, round felt hat and shaggy beard. He looked, indeed, more fit to grace one of those Hoys, lying just inshore with a free cargo, than a chairman at a Methody meeting, and one would hardly have been surprised had he " taken the Chair " with a cutlass between his teeth ! All he needed to complete the picture was a black patch over one eye. However, he was in truth a highly respectable member of the village community ; farmer-cum-fisherman-cum-hawker, and a worthy stalwart at the chapel ! And he was providing the horse and trap.

The way led through our Ford, and the colt was young and spirity. As they approached the water, they could just make out the shadowy forms of two men with a cart on the opposite side of the Ford, but wrong side of the road. Just as they landed in the middle of the water, a large and ferocious dog jumped at the colt's nose, barking furiously and trying to snap.

" Get out, yar brute ! Hare, carl yar dawg orf, wal yar ! and move yar cart, for yar on the wrong side o' road. We dont warnt tew be upset in this hare warter ; weer got a young cowt hare and tew wimmen in the back ! "

There were plungings, splashings, swervings, and all but an unwelcome bath, with a strong inclination on the part of the colt to go down-stream, until control was established and the other side reached, with a great sigh of relief on the part of all in the trap.

John said he " fared right riled thet he felt so narvous, but then yew niver knows what them young hosses 'ull dew ! "

But that was only the beginnings. A little " fudder,"

an old man popped out of a gateway, startling the
pony ; then two old cronies carrying hand lamps, then
one o' them spidery owd bikes raced past. Next four
or five old horses, part of a caravan, feeding beside the
road, seemed to sneeze right in the colt's ears ; until
finally, passing a farm, another dog rushed out into the
road and seemed as though it would devour colt, trap
and occupants in its fury. However, the village was
reached at last and a good congregation received the
travellers, with much clapping of hands, so that soon
the speakers got to speaking. This, set in an atmosphere of a country chapel as picturesque as the
congregation and the platform.

Imagine then, a long building with a gallery all round ;
box-like pews, made for " hosses " rather than people ;
singers' seats behind pulpit, but the latter placed in such
a way that it was an adventure for the preacher to reach
it. This was done by going up some steps, lifting up
some of the seats, then down other steps to land in a
manger that would hold not one preacher but four !

John was in reminiscent mood that night ; maybe the
result of the jerky journey and the uncertainty of the
return. He recalled the days when he first preached
there. No one remaining who was there then and so on.
All of which was received with great fervour by young
and old alike and they sang, almost shouted,—

> We're marching through Immanuel's ground,
> And soon shall hear the trumpet sound,
> And there we shall with Jesus reign,
> And never, never part again.
> What, never part again ?   (women)
> No, never part again !   (men)

But the old roof had stood a good deal and remained firm.

And so they turned for home ; bowling along the
dusty road, between the trees, under the stars, clacking
away to the ring of the hoofs, until the colt put itself
into a regular lather, even on so cold a night.

John could recall the days, as yesterday, full of the fear of Napoleon, and the tales told by his father and uncles of the coast watching. How you mustn't light so much as a match when you were atop the cliff. Perhaps it was as well, for they may have been even larger matches than those in the candlestick in his bedroom ; and assuming that Boney couldn't have seen the spluttering flame, well he could have smelt 'em ! Show, where as a boy, he was going to hide himself if any other would-be invader came, thereby evincing an unconscious fear handed down to him by Danish and Saxon ancestors. Mind the day when the railway crept up from Ipswich and "tunned" the Coaches off the turnpike. The Blue was a smart little turn-out that used to call at the Tuns at Yoxford. And sometimes you could just catch the note of the horn, as it made off for Lowestoft and Yarmouth. Yes, the railway made a good deal of difference ; not only tearing a way across the fields, but tearing a way through customs and conventions ; and "them owd crossin' gates" were a far greater nuisance than the toll-gates. They'd caused a deal of accidents, that they had ! witness the following conversation between our ear-ringed friend and the Prophet. It almost looked as though the tan had turned to sallow !

" Ha yar heerd the news, John ? "

" No, that I haint, Partner ! "

" Well, Sperry Free and young Baldry wer' a comin' home from Saxmundham, by North Green way, past Rainer's. The Gates wer' open fur the six o'clock train, then a coming, and Sperry ran right into it and wer' cut tew pieces. Sperry wer took down the line seventy yards or more, the hoss cut tew pieces but the boy wor thrown clear.

" It appears that Sperry and Baldry wer' a tryin' tew race Eaves and someone else in his cart, both on em tryin' tew get in front o' tother. Sperry wer' a leading

and drivin' that furious he didn' notice wher' he wor a
gooin'; didn't see the gates and as he touched 'em so
thay flew ope and the train caught him, cart and all.
Frank Spalding were out a drivin' his sister, said they
passed them a few minutes afore and hed tew draw
into a gateway tew let 'em pass. He say if they wornt
drunk, then it's a rum thing. That wer' some mess
and the stink tarrible ! Poor ole Sperry, I reckon he
went full gallop tew hell ! "

" Thar, thar. Mercy on us. I ollust knew he 'udn't
com' t' any good ; he war a rare soaker, though he never
did me any harm and somehow I ullus did like him. I
never thowt as how he'd go like that ; but, there were
ullus more of Sampson than of Solomon in him ; that
ther' wer'. And that wer' a right good little mare
tew ; she war whooly a warker, that she war ! "

Sussanah was the first to go the way of all flesh, and
terrible to him was the day when she died. She slipped
away as she had lived, quietly, without demonstration
and with the faintest semblance of a smile on her lips.
No more for her the " rough old road " to try her feet ;
the bitter blast at the chapel corner, or the wild
winds of winter to make her feel " right scared " as
they whined about her broad-bosomed chimney. In
that hour he was bereft of the restraining influences of
which he had so great need ; except that that other
restrainer was hard on his track—anno domini—which
doth turn lions into lambs.

They could not coffin her upstairs, because of that
evil little ladder of a staircase, so they brought her down,
once only to rest in state amongst the " likenesses "
and the turkey twill. To sleep against the lullaby
supplied by John Bright, Saxmundham, which was
not so much a clock as a sentinel of that time of which
death is but an incident. And they took her up the
Back-road Hill, in one of those carts with a detachable
seat, covered up with an old horse rug, to be buried

just under the flint wall with its lichened rounded-brick top, close to aunt Mahala, and hard by uncle Chambers.

He stayed on at the now empty farm. His inclination being to hasten home as quickly as possible in an endeavour to retrieve the loneliness which he imposed on her, whose mantle had now fallen on him. But the time for retirement. drew near and his place to be taken by a younger man. He moved to the thatched homestead set on the top of the hill as you go to the Yew Tree, to fill in the remaining years with a little peddling and a weekly visit to the market. Even chapel activities grew less and less, with his seat in the pew never vacant and his place in the pulpit never filled ; while his eyes on the rising generation were full of misgivings and doubts, summed up in the expression,— " The old uns can't, and the young uns 'ont ! "

His passing was by means of his chest ; difficult, stertorous ; as great a contrast to his Sussanah's end, as his life was to hers. And they sang over his coffin as it was lowered to join that sandy level of the copyhold the lines they sang at Wenhaston on that cold and moonlit night,—

> And there we shall with Jesus reign,
> And never, never part again.
> What, never part again ?
> No, never part again !

E

OWD GAL

In a close lane as I pursu'd my journey,
I spy'd a wrinkled hag, with age grown double,
Picking dry sticks, and mumbling to herself.
Her eyes with scalding rheum were gall'd and red ;
Cold palsy shook her head ; her hands seem'd wither'd :
And on her crooked shoulders had she wrapt
The tattered remnants of an old strip'd hanging,
Which served to keep her carcase from the cold :
So there was nothing of a piece about her,
Her lower weeds were all o'er coarsely patch'd
With different coloured rags, black, red, white, yellow,
And seem'd to speak variety of wretchedness.

Otway.

In telling of one one must tell of three, for they lived
together, a life of mutual interdependence. But,
perhaps, it would be more correct to say that the two
relied on the one, rather than the one on the two ;
for, in short, she ruled her two brothers with a rod of
iron ; the iron in this case being " her owd clack."
The fact of being their housekeeper was a mere side
issue ; but then as the saying goes—" If the hen does
not prate, she will not lay." They lived in the other
half of the two-dweller, as neighbour to the Prophet
and Sussanah.

Polly was a " quare " bundle ; as ongain a one as
Suffolk could produce ; out of the past of witches and
familiar spirits, into the years of that generation before
this, which was so much nearer to Elizabethan England
and witchcraft than we ; for our one brief span
has increased the gap beyond all proportion of its
years.

Of middling height, slightly bent, with two beady eyes
holding a slight squint ; eyes that seldom looked you
straight in the face, more often they crept past you, as
though, yes, as though you were not there. Her clothes

were part of her, and with that round piece of millinery, appeared, Minerva-like, to have entered life with her. Certainly she had no need of a wardrobe, or the little blind closet upstairs in which to keep her clothes.

Needless to say, it was a difficult matter to cultivate her acquaintance, for she was " ullus scrabbinabout at suffen " ; besides, she had no desire to have her affairs enquired into. She had enough to do to get a bit o' wittles ready for poor dear brother Tom and brother Fred to put in their " wittle-poke " for nunetimes. And what with baking and cleaning (you might have been a bit sceptical about the cleaning) there " wornt much time to mardle about." Then " there wor thet grut owd killer of a tub tew scalt out, and the spickets and fansets, for she wor a goin' tew brew tomorrow, for there wornt nowt but drigs in the cask. And poor brother Fred and poor brother Tom got thet dry wi' the sun a porin' down on thar backs in the harvest field, for thet wor sum hard wurk, thet thet wur."

Her life was full in a muddly, shuffling sort of way ; a sort of " backus " existence, with no time to sit in the " keep-room," if she had one. And it is quite certain you wouldn't get past the ground floor, however " thick " you might get ; but that floor was an interesting revelation in itself.

An ordinary Suffolk cottage, untouched by any wave of restoration ; with a front room, the major portion of which was occupied by the chimney, the mantel littered with bric-à-brac reminiscent of a Morland interior. Chairs and tables, with their legs carefully wrapped up in bulging pieces of paper, lest those " grut owd butes " should harm their polished surfaces. Pot-plants in the window overflowing to table and floor, to which she administered a drop o' tay occasionally ; while a few used cups and glasses filled up any open spaces that remained on the table. A general air of untidiness pervaded the whole, centreing about the old fire-place,

and the hob, on which the kettle lived a continuous life
of boiling and the pot of simmering.

Then, of course, there was the " backus," over " ta
trosshle " of which " trapsed them owd ducks and hins "
in their ever search for food. " Gew yew out dew ! "
Through this door of two parts, she trapsed herself a
thousand times a day, with her old steel-ringed pattens
clipping on the stones ; backwards and forwards to the
pump or to the shed.   Here, in this backus she washed,
baked, brewed. And her short-cakes and rusks were
not to be despised, nor the little loaves of bread that
lasted fresh for nine or ten days, even if they did get
mixed up with a little ash and dust in the making. But
then it was a rare business baking, the backus full of
faggots, the lower half of the wicket door closed to
keep out them " owd hins " and " hoppen-toads," and
the top part open to let in a little more light and to let
out the smoke and the steam. But " my haart, that
wer a good smell ! "— wood fire mixed up with the
baking and an occasional whiff of frizzling pork !

Here, too, was a little " owd " cupboard, " wi' one
gimmer broke," that that " owd worrit " of a dealer
wanted to buy. " That belonged tew me poor dear
mother, that did ; come off the Moor years and years
ago. She say it wer made by them owd monks at
Leiston Abbey."

" I wonder what he want thet for ? That aint no
mander o'. good, that aint, but he shant hev it, no he
shant ! "

And then the larder, which amounted in area to
another small room, and was full of all " mander o'
things."   Maybe a bit of Lowestoft, or Wedgwood
black ware, or mugs with gay rings, mixed up with
things done up in rough paper parcels. An old rusty
jack, stuck in the corner. A few wicker baskets, worm-
eaten and powdery. Bottles, stone and glass, dusty
and smelling of long-lost contents ; a broken pie-pan,

broken parts of a clock. All carefully preserved, as though some day they would become whole again at a general and useful resurrection.

Polly had her distinct aversions, for she was of the objective variety ; a " scuppit " was a " scuppit " to her and not a spade. One of these was the doctor, for she " wornt a goin' tew make hare innards into a chimists shop, thet she wornt ; non o' his jalop for her or his owd pills ! " And when Tom came home with the " pin-o'-his-throat " a bit loose like, she knew what to give him ; and she saw to it that they didn't sit about wet shod, those two, when they came home from ploughing or muck carting. He was a nice enough kind-hearted gentleman, for he wor some kind to her poor dear mother when she wor struck wi death. But she didn't warnt anything tew dew wi' him harself or his owd medicine. Besides, what wer wrong wi' a wineglassful o' Verdock root water, boiled wiout brakin' the skin? That taken every second day for a week or two 'ud put yew right, thet it wud ! And when poor brother Fred's feet wer' thet sore he could hardly hobble up and along the ten-acre field, she made him take off his shoes and stockings and stand in his bare feet in the horses' water, what used to collect in that little owd dip in the stables. " Thet cured him, thet did ! "

Next in order of aversion was the Rector, not forgetting his wife. "What roight 'a they got a coming hare talkin' about fresh air, and falals and fancies o' thet sart ? " And " doant I think it wud be a gude idee if I kep the owd hog a bit fudder from the backus door ? Why thet owd sty took a mort o' time tew build, and thet hev been admired, yes thet sartainly hev. Brother Fred built thet when we coomed hare, tharty yare agoo cum Michaelmas ; and I mind when poor Tom got a bit light hidded and plumpandikkalla'd right into the muck from his bedroom window. My haart, he whooly scared the owd sow ! No, we doant wornt any o'

Parson's ideas, let him keep them fur his cellar what
fill itself wi Rachfur and smell suffin awful ! "

Polly hadn't got much of an idea about " ta Maaster "
either, but she dussent shew it too much. He wor one
o' they jumped up like people, not like " ta owd maaster."
Lives like owd Pamp half the week and then goes
jackety-pinch for the rest. " Coom hare on his hoss with
his mimmixin' sart o' way, marndarin' an' garpin' at
us as ta sayen is. Besides, if he cud dock a bit o' pay
off poor Tom's wages he would ; and he's thet mean
about the glanin'. He wouldn't leave'n more'n then
a hen's nose full, if he could help it. As for his bier ;
why, thet be pizen'd wi' water ! "

And yet she was a good neighbour, always willing to
do a hand's turn for poor Sussanah, next door. Poor
dear crittur, with her bad head and poor eyes. Although
it's true, Sussanah was not too anxious to avail herself
of the help ; while John was fearful that the Suffolk
interior from next door might find its way into his half
of the two-dweller !

Tom, by the way, was the eldest of the three and a
little bit simple. He had evidently been born in the
chime hours (8—12—4) and must have " sucked the
silly side of his mother ! " He was below middle stature
in height, bow-legged, the legs encased in very ancient
buskins, and walked abroad carrying a stick cut out
of the hedgerow. Bald, by a constant wearing of the
faded billy-cock hat, with its wavy greasy line at the
junction of crown and brim ; but if he did have occasion
to lift off this hat which seemed to be a part of himself,
then his shiny crown glowed strangely white against
the general tan of his face. He had a short but tously
little beard, eyes as evasive as those of his sister, and a
habit of wagging his head, either from side to side or up
and down, and of constantly mumbling to himself ;
added to this a short sharp little walk that almost went
into a trot. He certainly looked and acted a bit queer,

and the children saw to it that they kept out of his way and dared not call after him. Besides; wearing a sackas apron and waving his knives, when he was about to kill the hog, left a nasty picture in the mind that needed no colouring. And it was with almost fiendish glee that he dragged the sow's carcass to the little low stool to cut it up with that special narrow sharp knife that so effectually did its work.

His madness came in cycles and took the form of religious doubts and fears. He could see they little devils sitting about the room or putting stuff in his tea; trying to get him to their hell! Then it was that Polly was at her best, and humoured him back, out of his fears, to the amity of life as lived by them. His life was also hemmed in by a great fear that it might end in the "House." The spectre of Bulcamp sent a cold shiver down most spines.

On the farm he was the cowman, and twice a day was to be seen on his way to the marshes calling home the cows. Funny owd things, they cows; sometimes they'd be near the gate waiting for him, another time they couldn't seem to get far enough away, right over agin they popples. He then would stand and "holler" as loud as he could "Coupee, Coupee," and sometimes they'd come and sometimes they udn't!

His favourite pastime was pritching for eels, and he could tell rare tales of the river; its floods and caprices, and of the hole where the tumbrel and horses were lost; not because of the size of the hole or the depth of the river, but because "owd Mother Lumpkin cromed 'em in." But then also he knew the haunt of wild fowl, where you were likely to hook a pike with a ligger at night, or strike an owd harnser. And if you were careful and anxious, show you a green-shank; but you'd have to almost "howd yare breath!" But he never went near the river when his queer fits came on, for Jack-o'-Lanterns and mermen were too real; and a nest of plovers' eggs weren't worth the risk of being cromed into the water, never to come out again.

Fred, on the other hand, was a jovial red-faced, agreeable fellow, who looked after the horses. A pleasant, vacuous son of the soil, but by far the most human of the three. The study in contrasts that belongs to so many families. Clean shaven, but for a moustache, which cleanliness must be taken in a relative rather than absolute sense, since the shaving was a weekly event— Saturday night to be exact—and therefore the chin was like the fields after reaping—a bit stubbly with white bristles.

His eyes were far franker than those of his brother and sister, though in their blueness they carried that far-seeing look of the sea or wide fields—fields before the enclosure. He wore the carter's smock down to his hips, possessed a magnificent mole-skin waistcoat for Sundays, and sometimes wore an old blue coat over his smock, the legacy of a yeoman of a generation before. But it looked a smart turn-out when he went to the Bell, or a chapel meeting, where he always sat in the gallery, leaning over the little rail. But he knew how to manage horses, and could bring a shine into their coats and a gloss into their long tails and manes ; and the bits of brass on their harness shone like gold. And he knew they could see ghosts ; that was why they " ullus shied when they went past that crooked bit of an old ellum at the top of the ten-acre." "Thet wur where owd Betsy Backus had hung herself. They'd buried hare owd carcass, but hare spirit couldna' settle ! "

Starting out at day-break most mornings, riding side saddle in that rhythmical swaying motion, stirring up the dust as he swung out of the gate, carrying his elevenses in that old straw bag, up and down the furrows, ploughing or harrowing all day, how many miles would he walk, think ye ? And, if you listen, following the hedge along the ten-acre, you can still hear his cuppey-whey, woosh, com-hather, or tarn-ye ! see the dust flying from the fetlocks of his Punches—Captain and Darkie—and smell the sweet flavour of new-turned earth.

But should you have run into him, with his straw in his mouth, and should you have said, " That owd hoss is tender on the wallis," or " She be wos this marning," he would reply, " Yes, yes." Or should you say, " I dont hode wi' all this parlarvarin about New Orders," he would answer, " No, no " ; stand and smile broadly, move the straw from one side of his mouth to the other ; answer you always with " yes, yes," or " no, no," and then plod on until " closing in time," with the prospect of " suffin hot " on his return home.

And these three made home together ; killed a pig now and then ; saw to it it was killed at the waxing and not the waning of the moon—to save the flesh from shrinking in the curing and the cooking. (But then, we were rare followers of the moon in Suffolk, for the winter wheat must be sown in October or November at the new moon, to grow with it.) Hung a ham or two and some chaps up that capacious chimney ; had what they needed of drink and " wittals," bread and short-cakes, a cask of key-beer once a year ; never bathed, yet were not dirty, and " ullas paid their rent come Michaelmas." Not your Michaelmas, oh, no, but the real Suffolk Michaelmas of October the eleventh. They succeeded, too, in keeping everyone at arm's length ; preferred old times to new ; had no relations and saw to it they didn't make any new ones. In short, they were as self-contained as three people in one small cottage could be ; taking no account of the " cackle of the bourg."

They would sit round that glowing wood fire in the longest nights of winter, with a strange capacity of staring into its depths, to the side of which were one or two iron implements ; a flat toasting iron, one of those curved rakers used for baked potatoes, a three-pronged wire toasting fork and a skillet, with the "kitling" right in front of the blaze. That kitling was a rare good weather chart for as she washed herself you knew of wet or fine. The doorways, for there were two, one into the front garden, the other into the backus, were, with the windows, heavily hung with sacks to keep out the slightest draught or the least bit of air. And they would have little to say, only their bodily presences conveying any sensations to one another. Tom's hands hanging loose from the wrists, with occasional flickings of the fingers, his eyes wandering from fire to floor. Polly, with heavily-mittened fingers, sipping a rusk soaked in tea ; spooning it with a luscious suction ; and Fred, twitching his feet on the brick floor, littered as it was with bits of firing ; thinking of Darkie over the other side of the yard. The darkness of the room faintly lit by a rushlight held slantwise in the holder, the glow of the fire giving almost sufficient light until the tallow candles were lit for bed. After all, they had no need of brighter illumination, for they could not read, neither for that matter had they anything to read were they able. No clock to guide them in the dark mornings as to when to rise, yet they always knew the time, and if in any doubt, could tell by looking out of the tiny latticed windows and noting the stars, especially just where the Plough happened to be. Besides, there was always John next door ; they could hear him moving about and singing, in that somewhat tremulous tone—" Awake my soul and with the sun "—with which he always started the day. The tune seemed to consist of verbs and nouns, with only a faint connection of adjectives and adverbs, much like the efforts on his horn in the band. Perchance they might talk a little of past years, of the " furmety " mother used to make on Christmas Eve, and sometimes, given light enough, Polly would do a bit of mending, and Fred a little straw plaiting for a bag, or a mat for the backus door.

Polly, with her twitching eyes and high-pitched sing-song voice, in a conversation plentifully interlarded with " poor dear," and a shaking of her head. Tom, with a mumbling undertone in a deeper key, and Fred, seldom other than to agree—life being too short to disagree or in the least to complain. And so they would sit, happy in their self-sufficiency, perhaps the wind roaring about the chimney, whistling through the tree tops ; and in moments of quiet, the dull roar of the sea across the Walks, denoting as Polly said, with awe, " the sea ha' gort it " ; " it " being the tempest. Or, maybe, the rain, pouring in torrents, with occasional splashes, falling down the straight shaft, spitting like some old serpent out of the burning embers.

Of course, it was only in winter that any sort of homelife was lived at all. Every scrap of daylight, and much of dark, was used in some sort of work either in garden, shed, or allotment. And they would come in to snatch a few mouthfuls of food, mostly bread and onions, washed down with beer, and then off to bed, to get ready for the morning.

And so they lived, year in and year out, with a complete absence of self analysis, and for that matter of self absorption. Doing the same things in the same way, and finding no dullness in the repetition and the round. Using the same tools as father and grandfather, with life punctuated by Michaelmas and Easter. Sowing and reaping, with seldom a high-day to mark any divisions, save the Horkeys at Harvest, or a day on Parson's meadow to mark some national event that was insignificant enough as far as they were concerned. The night when Rouse's mill caught fire at Westleton, and the old sails burnt like a catherine wheel, was of far more importance and stood out in vivid detail in their horizon. And there were days to remember in the

Rackford floods that crept higher and higher along the road to the parson's meadow, and all the marshes under water with the poplars standing out like masts of a sunken wreck. With tales of shipwrecks off Dunwich, or Aldeburgh, to filter slowly through from lip to lip, losing nothing in the telling, nor indeed capable of much loss in the terror and the heroism which they called forth. They were out of the soil, and one day, in God's good time, they would return to the soil, and they were content, thankful for a good master, dully tolerant of a bad one.

But the longest life and the most contained ends and breaks at some time or another. Not much of ill had come their way ; save the agueing fever which made itself felt now and again. They had escaped accidents in the harvest field and small-pox ; the only disability appearing periodically in poor Tom, which always seemed to coincide with the moon, and lasted for a matter of a week at the most. As for coughs and rheumatism, well they could be short-circuited by a little rum—there was a bottle in the pantry and you needn't ask how it got there—or a special bottle of Polly's wine, elder to wit. And what was the matter with a good pie-pan full of onion gruel afore you went to bed, added to the rum !

But Tom's complaint was deeper seated than rum could reach. It was of the wind that howled in the chimney, or the rain that hissed in the fire, or the force that broke the schooners on the Shipwash, and tore the trees from their roots and split them as you would a pig in the butchering. Neither John's Methodism nor the parson's Prayer-book had any effect, and only Polly could humour it out of him. You would have thought from the sing-song prating that her spell would have acted quite otherwise, adding fuel to the fire like the shanny brains and empty chatterings of some women with weak-minded men ; but there was power behind the squint, power akin to the spirit that troubled poor Tom. And as Tom grew older, not so old as men count years, the evil troubled him the more, and with the fall of the year, as befitted one who was of the soil and the fields, he died, with fear in his eyes, and the cold beads of fear on his clammy tanned forehead. Tossing and turning in his narrow bed, imploring sister to keep off the evil ones who haunted his crazy mind ; until friend death, who, having lingered on those crooked stairs, knocked at the already open door, strode silently in, and gave rest to such unquiet. While the old dog had been howling for the best part of the night, right under the bedroom window. And dogs " ullus " know !

Then, but not too soon, followed Polly ; crawling about to the very last. Should Fred call the doctor ? By no means, she had no use for him in life, why then should he trouble her in death ? which she preferred to masquerade as life. Besides, she couldn't abide the flash of his gig, or the jingle it made along the road. Until at last her legs gave way, and she was forced to take to bed. Kindly, quiet old Sussanah was then called in, who opened the way for the doctor, and Polly knew her time had come.

Old Bailey, as he was familiarly called, was a kind-hearted country practitioner, who doctored in the teeth of the weather, with a limited pharmacopœia, and a blind eye to recompense. He failed no one, squire or labourer, or that " mawther " of a wench who had twins afore she ought. 'Tis true, he had more geese at Michaelmas than he knew what to do with, but they served as a prophylactic against any outbreak of fees. He met everyone on an equal footing, talked no " furrin " language, but the rich jargon of old Suffolk, poured out in mutual comfort.

He had dosed a good many " quare " patients, but never one quite so queer as old Polly, whom he knew well from a back view, and by report, though not face to face.

" How d'ye howd now, old gal? " was his kindly
enquiry.

" Thank 'e, maaster, wery mahderate; I fare a bit
duzzy, loike ! "

" Any pain? "

" Iss, no."

But beyond that he could not go. He might look at
her tongue, but he couldn't look into her " hid," or by
her pulse probe into the windings of her thoughts.
Questions led to evasions, born of cunning and fear, and
he realised that only a necromancer could diagnose or
find the cure. However, that did not prevent him
calling, for he had a rare love for his fellows, and here
was a rich field of interest if he could only plumb its
depths.

And so she died, as inscrutably as she had lived, with
a sardonic smile spread over the shrunken mask of her
face, while the squint seemed to spread from the huddled
bed to every part of the tiny chamber. She had tricked
them all, as she always meant to do, and died of cancer
with no one the wiser. But with all her apparent
untidiness and disregard of appearances and people, she
was anxious after respectability, especially the respectability of burial, and they found, tucked away in the
grubby depths of the mattress, amid the clutter accumulated in and on the bed, a little store of sovereigns,
which she had secured in her careful secretiveness against
the day when she should be " took up the Back-road
hill " to join the others. And if any sacrilegious hand
had turned that gold to another channel, then her squint
would follow them remorselessly, until they lost it and
themselves, in the river !

So, out of the wrack of time, Fred was left to face the
world alone, in advanced middle-age, with an empty
hearth. What should he do? Only two women had
entered into his life—his mother and Polly—and Polly
had been wife and mother to him through most of his

life. Who, then, should get his " wittals " ready ? his
elevenses and fourses ? Who brew his beer and bake
his bread ? and prate at him and call him " poor brother
Fred " behind his back ? " Hosses " are all very well,
but they cannot take the place of " wimmen " in the
life of a man nor make those savoury stews which his
soul loveth. Besides, the little house was strangely
empty, strangely quiet in a life of peace, forbiddingly
aggressive in its stirrings of memory, and his visits to the
Bell became more frequent, and sometimes he returned
homewards a little fuddled, not remembering when he
had passed Parson's meadow ; but it made him sleep
the better.

And it seemed to him that, after all, perhaps he had
better get married—take a chance on it ; " hitty-
missy " like. She was not a bad wench, that gal down
at the Valley Farm ; gave him a can of beer once when
he had gone there after stover, and called him " Fred,"
too. But that were a long time agoo ; besides, perhaps
she had got someone now, funny if she hadn't. But
" thar, thar," he'd make it his business to find out ;
and yet, how was he " a gooin' tew ? " Made him
scratch his head a good deal ; he'd taken off his hat more
in one day than ever before ; he'd catch cold, that he
would. He'd goo down there come Sunday, put on his
best blue coat and a clean smock—if he could find one—
and see wot he could see. Besides, he'd like tew see
them heifers at Joe King's corner, and then he could cut
through the Wash.

And he did. My heart, thet wer hot work. Thet
wer whooly scorching, the nearer he got to Valley Farm.
And would you believe it, they'd been and done away
with the owd thatch and put them owd tiles on instead.
Didn't somehow look the same ; but yes, there was the
old bullace trees, and the old apples, and the currant
bushes spreading nearer and nearer to the gate. And
there she wor, wud yew believe it, in luck's way, he wor,

and the old straw in his mouth seemed to move from side to side of its own accord. Should he speak fust ? No, he'd let her do that, and she did.

" Hullo, Fred. What be yew a dooin' right oova here ? Yew be a long way from hoome ! "

" Yes, yes," was all he could manage.

" Dew yew want tew see Maaster, or someun ? "

" No, no," came the reply.

" Wot, are yew jest out fur a walk ? "

" Yes, yes."

" Gooin tew Kelsale Bells ? "

" No, no."

" Round by the Moor ? "

" No, no."

And so it might have gone on till next harvest ; when, his face getting redder and redder, and the straw now moving faster and faster, he axed her—if she hadn't got anything better tew dew, whether she'd marry him, and come and look after his house for him ?

" Wot me ? Ada Foulcher ? Hev yew bin a drinkin', Fred, and doant know what yer'e a dooin ? "

" Yes, yes ; no, no ! " he exclaimed, mentally exhausted.

" Why, yew're old enough tew be my faather ; that yew are ! Rackun yew're drunk ! "

" No, no."

" Well, if yew aren't, I'll come, thet I 'ull."

And she did.

OWD BOR

Nay, I am not yet so mad or so blind,
For when I am at my cart or my plow
I am more merry than either of you,
I would not change my life nor my lyffyng
For to be made a great Lord or a Kyng.
....
....
But a man that can meanings find
To have food and cloths and a merry minde
And to desire no more than is needful
That is in this world the lyf most joyful.
                                                           1535.

PRESTON or " Pressy " Arnold lived alone, the last
survivor of an old yeoman family of these parts. Generations of Arnolds have left a name in the various parishes
about here, especially the ancient Borough, which now
lies under the grey waters of the North Sea—our old
port, and ancient capital city—Dunwich. Read its
story and you will soon trace the Arnolds in its maritime
history and its municipal pretensions, among " the
King's good men of Dunwich."

His house, large for one only person, is at the end of
the " Carnser " or Causeway—at the corner as you
turn to go to the Moor. A curious bit of Suffolk architecture, in its rambling collection of rooms, for it didn't
matter whether you approached from the front or the
back, the fact was that having passed through the best
room in the front or the kitchen parlour at the rear, you
came into a quite capacious hall, with a wide and
serviceable staircase that led upstairs to little rooms
running off in two directions. Evidently the place
had seen better days, had been added to by successive
owners, and was certainly the most deceitful bit of
brickwork in the parish. It was far larger than one
imagined from an exterior view.

81

F

In many respects the place, with its tiled roof, seemed to settle about Pressy in much the same manner as his hat on his head, or to have grown about him as his own clothes. It has been altered now beyond all recognition, and although imposing, rising sheer out of the grey green of the " maashes," yet it has lost its character—the character which it succeeded in bestowing on Preston.

Preston Arnold had one end and aim in life, which seemed to dominate him soon after mid-day, every day— to get ready for the morning. Summer and winter a fire burned in his grate and therefore the kindling must be got ready, and the kettle filled.

And what a kettle it was, made of copper, of huge dimensions for country thirsts, ten pints if it held a gill, and black with the continual smoke of countless fires. Its great heavy bar of a handle over its lid, which grew a copper acorn, the only clue that remained of its metal. The " wittals " prepared, the cup and saucer and plate ear-marked for the first meal of the day.

Pressy had learnt to do for himself long enough ago ; long before the loss of his wife, before even he knew her ; so that when he was called to face life alone, he was not shiftless. In fact, it might be said that he took a pride in his cooking, and no little pride in telling to anyone who would listen how this and that could be cooked and eaten. He was in fact a first-rate cook and pastry maker—give him a hare or pheasant, and see ! And you would want a large helping of one of his gooseberry tarts !

Then he fancied himself considerably over his wine making, which he experimented with and concocted in large and liberal quantities. Anything seemed to go into the distillation ; potatoes, apples, pears, raisins, wheat, sugar, parsnips, yeast ; until it was difficult to find a vessel large enough to contain the brew. And then he could make whisky—" Yes, he could, Bor "— but " dussent, cause he wur tew near the rood ! "

Perhaps it was as well he " dussent," for his wine was potent enough ; and as for his stout ; well, if it didn't upset you the first glass or two, then " yer innards " were proof against anything.

" Hev a glass o' wine ? " was his first and most insistent greeting, when you set foot in his muddled kitchen. And you, being unawares, would find yourself with a tumbler full ! A tumbler taken off the shelf and dusted with finger and thumb, and then filled from an old stone bottle. After a mouthful or two, you would begin to forget you were in his kitchen ; his old sing-song voice would become more and more distant, until you were firmly of the opinion that, somehow or other, you were in a tubular-shaped room, Preston Arnold at one end and you at the other !

His wife, of whom he seldom spoke, had passed out per an old motor tyre. No, not " runned " over, as you might imagine. It was like this. The fortnightly baking had come round again, and always on the look-out for fuel for the oven, she had acquired a discarded tyre for the purpose. " Thet whooly roared when thet got gooin', my haart it did " ; and she, anxious to see if the oven was hot enough, unwittingly opened the furnace door. It was the old story of the Old Testament re-enacted, but in this case it was the innocent actor in the drama who perished, licked up in the flames of her own making ; but her end was speedy.

After so sudden and unfortunate a death, Arnold was somewhat nonplussed as to what he should do. He was not uncomfortably off, and certainly possessed a comfortable home. Of one thing his mind was clear, he would not marry again ; the solution therefore seemed to lie in a housekeeper of some kind or another to look after him ; and after all, Susan " ud dew his warshin' fur un."

For a time he endured the services of a relative ; twenty stone in weight if she was a pound ; but what she made up for in bulk she lacked in ballast, and he was soon disconcerted with her light-headed ways. As he said, she " ullus reminded him of the owd saying "—

> Said the Chevin to the Trout,
> My head's worth all thy bouk.

So when she went on a visit to another relative and did not return, he was greatly relieved.

Then he thought he might get someone daily for a bit, which was how he came by young Kate. She could do a bit of " clanin'," sweeping, dusting and a bit of washing, peel the potatoes and mend his shirt. One day he marched in with a hare secreted in one of the large pockets of his coat. " Thare yew be," he exclaimed as he threw it on the backus floor. " Can yew cook a hare ? " But Kate, if she was a bit simple, wasn't to be caught like that.

" Well, me mother could," she replied.

He thought that was a good tidy answer, so he proceeded to cook the " blamed " thing himself. " I stuffed he wi' onions, sage and a few little things out o' the hedge, made the oven good tidily warm, covered his owd carcase with some pastry, and my wud, he fared sum good !"

But Arnold was not quite alone. First there was his glossy-coated spaniel bitch, that never moved far from his feet. In fact, her devotion had well nigh been her undoing, for when he was scything his " little owd pightle," she got in his way and he ripped open her belly, as in a twink ! But, of course, he hadn't had a little " vet " training for nothing, so he wrapped her up in a sack, carried her home like a babe, and just sewed the flabby flesh together. And that was that !

But with all her devotion, she was, unfortunately, a thief ; she was not to be trusted where food was concerned, and she had an intimate knowledge of what was in the larder. Thrashings had no effect in deterring her depredations should an opportunity occur. And this was not confined to things of her master.

" Ha yew got yare piece of beef alright ? " asked Arnold of one of his neighbours.

" Yes, thankee," replied she, wondering what he was after.

" Well, dew yew goo and look." And sure enough it had gone.

But Arnold always paid for Bessy's raids, though sometimes the price was a little more than the prime cost. But he knew ; there wasn't much he didn't, and he only grinned.

Then there were his cats, thin faced and wild looking, but they kept the rats and mice down, even if they were always having kittens. They lived in that box just inside the fender.

In fact, Arnold was never without, nor never had been without companionship of birds or animals of one kind or another. At one time it was a couple of fox cubs he had reared into comparatively tame foxes ; but they weren't looked upon with too kindly eyes by the neighbours.

Then there was the occasion when he set an old hen on a clutch of duck's eggs, from which only one duckling resulted. Judging this to be a waste of maternity, he turned the solitary fledgling into the care of the cat which had just had kittens, with strange and happy results. The old cat took to her new progeny, fostered it to the very best of her ability until the two became almost inseparable. Trapesing about the garden together they became a nuisance so Arnold turned the duck into the chicken run, to discover later, with regret, that the fowls had harried it to death !

In his early years there was some talk of Arnold becoming a " Vet." One of his uncles followed this vocation and Arnold received a smattering of learning in this direction, which, with his natural ability and aptitude with birds and animals, stood him in good stead. He knew their little ways, understood their secrets, and they seemed to take it for granted that he knew and responded accordingly.

It was so with the hawk that the squire kept in a cage at the Hall. Arnold could do most things with it, including moving the cage with the bird inside. One of the outdoor servants, thinking he could do the same, essayed to grip the cage, whereupon the bird gripped his hands, and dug his talons into the flesh so that it was difficult to disengage claw from hand ; but it was Arnold who did it. It was the same with the young bull. Arnold could manage him as well as he could manage Bessy or his old cats.

For more years than he cared to tell, Arnold drove the mail cart from Dunwich to Saxmundham, putting up for the night at the latter place, and returning the next morning. In all weathers, at all seasons, meeting all kinds of people, it was a job not without interest. Across Westleton Heath, purple in summer, a snowy waste in winter, his way was marked not so much by milestones as by trees ; that row of " old ellums " just above Westleton, the deep cluster that denoted Dunwich and the Squire's estate on the return journey. To say nothing of the sky, with its softness over the water, and the billowing beauty as you turned inland. His old " hoss " knew every inch of the way, could even keep the road when that was blotted out by snow, as his master knew every mother's son he passed on that way ; and people could set their clocks as the little old red cart trotted by. And if he did put up at an inn, and if he did meet all sorts of people, it was only once that he fell from grace ; and that was owing to the artfulness of a commercial. How he got home he didn't quite remember, but " my haart, he wer thet queer."

But the chief attraction about Preston Arnold was his

home. Littered and cluttered about were all kinds of things which he had picked up along life's way, or had been handed down. For instance, in his kitchen was the old table, as interesting a bit of craftsmanship as you would meet in a day's hunting. It had followed him about from place to place, had been held in no esteem whatsoever, had had an ugly excrescence of a drawer fastened to the underside of its top on one side, and supported many a " stun " of flour in the days when the old mills had twizzled their sails when the wind allowed. It was a refectory table, with a top of planks some two to three inches thick and was supported with rough-hewn ends pegged together by wooden pegs. Hand smooth with age and wear, it had probably come out of the monastery at Dunwich or the Abbey at Leiston.

In his front room were all kinds of things. A fine mahogany table in three parts, supported and surrounded by a set of six chairs of the same wood that had come from some local chair maker, long since dead. In the cupboards, set in the recesses, were lustre jugs, pieces of cut glass, old silver, and various bric-à-brac that he had collected from various auctions that he had attended. In entirety, as in detail, a complete and satisfying country home that all might envy, as indeed many did. An artless collection of the antique and the beautiful.

Being sometimes lonely, he was hospitable and only too anxious to receive anyone who might grace him with a visit. Besides it was something to be the possessor of things which raised envy in other people. And somehow or other, people did come. He would show them this or that, let them wander where they liked, handle anything with the utmost carelessness. Tell them how he got this at such and such ; and, " what dew you think on it ? I don't fare tew care for't much." But always end up with the same definite decision. " I 'ont sell ! "

The table in the kitchen was the *pièce de résistance*. " My haart it ud whooly stamm yer, if I told yew what I've been bid fur thet." One man was so anxious that he offered to buy it, pay the money there and then and leave it with Arnold for the rest of his life. " Luvlee owd table, thet be," as he caressed it with his hand. " I didn't think much on't, until Mrs. Jones come hare and begged and plagued me tew let her hev it. No, I says, I 'ont dew thet ; that look nice in my owd kitchin, I'd miss thet if thet wer gone, and thet belonged tew my poor owd mother. Thet's some old, thet thet is ; and when I giv thet a dewin' with a drop of linseed thet whooly shines. Not much linseed, but a mort o' rubbin' and yew can see yare face in't. I mind the time when thet stood up in the corner of our owd kitchen at home, piled up wi' sacks o' flour or meal ; we didn' pay no regard tew thet."

And so it was with his pictures, or his jugs or the Paisley shawl, " yew can look at em, but I ont sell. Time enough fur thet when I'm gone ; yew together can hev em then if yare lucky ! I don't pay no regard to them, but I ont sell." And he meant what he said. And who shall say that he was wrong ? They constituted in their diversity and in their beauty, his home. This little old grog-table, this coffin stool, this broken-down grandfather's clock ! And it would have been a poor substitute, a few pounds done up in a bag, tucked away under his bed, or housed in the coldness of a bank ! Besides, if they went, perhaps the callers would vanish too ; and there was a deal of satisfaction in possessing things that other folks coveted. He liked to watch their expressions and hear what they had to say, and he was always willing to give them a glass of his wine. But however long the bargaining, however artful the would-be owner, it always ended with the same tantalising words,—" I ont sell ! "

But above and beyond his house and his widowhood,

was his garden and his bit of land. He would grow more peas and " taters " than he knew what to do with, but he could " ullus " give 'em away. Not forgetting his pots of geraniums that he kept in the shelter of the kitchen window. Prize geraniums they were for he always figured in the flower shows and always brought home several of the prizes. Used to give those geraniums a little drop of tea, and a pinch of ammonia. Had to be careful, but it was wonderful how they liked it and freshened themselves up, if you didn't give 'em too much. And so with his eggs, his rabbits and his hens. As for his bit of garden, it was a mixture of flowers and vegetables, half and half kind of thing, so there was always something for the bees to be busy over, for he always kept a " skep or two for they," just the other side of the " shod." And when they swarmed they didn't seem to want to go far from the old garden, except when they must needs go off and fasten themselves on the chapel pulpit because the doors happened to be opened for the service and the Prophet had to delay the preaching until Pressy came and bagged them. Generally speaking they seemed to know when they were in a good home with a good keeper !

But he had one or two visitors besides the would-be purchasers, in the shape of two old men who often came in of evenings to make a hand at cards or talk of days long dead. The one a church-warden and bell ringer, the other a magnificent relic of a man, who must of necessity stoop low, which he did by instinct as well as perforce. A guardsman who might have served as a figure head to one of those old fighting ships in the Dunwich Roads ; or newly home from that " damned near thing " just across the water !

A glass of wine all round would act as enlivener— somehow or other the stout was always glossed over in a polite manner.

" Hev a glass o' wine, Scarlett ? "

" Thank ee, I doant mind if I dew."

And Arnold would reach for a grimy tumbler from the domed recess besides the fireplace.

" Yew doant mind hevin' the one yew hed last night ? "

" Noah, sartainly I doant ! "

" What about yew, Cady ? Hev some o' my stoot ? Made it'n yesterday."

" Noah, thank ee, I'll kep tew the wine, me innards 're a bit grumpey like."

And so they would fall to cards, and later to " mardlin."

Scarlett had been in sarvice to the old Squire and would recount little bits of reminiscences of the great families thereabouts.

" Did yew know how it wur that so-and-so hed tew tak up doctorin' ? "

" No, thet I didn't ; offen wondered why, tew ; he wur so fond o' hosses. Liked ridin' them a dale more than dosin' folks, I know ! "

" The old squire wur some fond o' him, tew ; ullus said he'd settle that nice little bit o' property, yew know, the Dower House they calls it, on him so's he could get in the Cavalry. But they'd forgot that artful cunning owd parson they had at the chuurch, then ; owd Scott, if yew recalls. Well, he used tew slip into the House after church on a Sunday evening and play a hand wi' the owd man. Then he managed tew push his daughter in, and well, it worn't very long afore Squire married the Parson's wench, and his nephew lost his chances wi' they hosses ; so he joined them rascals the doctors ; but he's still fond o' cowts. Tew books fur him they say,—Racin' Calender and Bible ! "

" Did yew hare that one about young C——, him that wuer in the Rifles ; yew know ? "

" Noah, I niver did rightly hare about thet. Left his regiment and went orf wi' a company o' singers, didn' he ? "

" Yes, well thet wur the owd lady's fault. Regular owd tartar she wur. Used tew make him an allowance and all thet, so when the war bruke out wi' they Boors, she wudn't let him go, not she. Made him get summun else tew take his place. They dew say the Adjitant went round one day and axed who of 'em wud like £200 and tew goo orf tew Africa instead of C. There wur a young orficer there who owed more than he could pay, and he could hardly believe his ears. He say, What ? could I dew with £200 ? Oh, my haart ! He jumped up right quick; I can tell ee. And when he coom hoome he had three medals as well as the money. Thet made poor little C——so savage and sick wi' hisself that he chucked up soldering and went off wi' they singers."

And so the tales would run. Arnold would tell how he cured owd Dix's cow that was a-choking, and how Dix wouldn't have it so, but they got the oil down the old cow's throat and she was soon right again. Or of days out with the Squire wildfowling. Red-letter days they were, " he whooly enjoyed them " ; when all the dykes were frozen hard ; " and yew hed tew wait all froze up yareself, fur yew niver knowed how them owd buds ud come ; whether they'd be out o' rach, left, right or slap overhid." But they never came home empty—not they, and Squire used to say—" goo yew and see the butler, Arnold, and axe him fur a bottle o' my port, and goo yew home and drink my health ! "

Or " dew yew remember poor owd George Easy ? "

" Should think I dew," asserted Cady. " Rare nice fella he wur, I mind tew when his boat went down off the Cache cliff and he wur pulled out by Lambert and tew o' his mates. He giv' they a telescope apiece fur thare trouble."

" Thet wur funny about him," squeaked Arnold, " when that photo fella used tew come and howd his spiritism meetin's. I used tew enjoy them right well. Funny thet wur ow thet little owd table 'ud cant about.

Poor owd George thowt he'd like tew goo tew one o' they. He wornt afraid a nawthin' he wornt, but when he got inside he coom'd over right queer. Thowt tew hisself, I must git out o' hare ; so he grabs up his hat as he thowt, puts it on his hid, and when he got outside he found as he wur a warin' owd Susan's bonnet. Laugh, I shud think we did. Sad thet wur when he got drownded ; but thare, thare, he ullus knew as how he wud some time or tother."

But so soon as the clock struck half nine, the three would part ; Arnold to get further ready for the morning, the other two to their respective beds ; silhouetted as they slowly moved against the evening sky which bade to be fair or " rokey " come to-morrow.

" Thets a tidy mist a comin' up orf them maashes, Cady ! "

" Yes, thet thet is."

" Thet ull be a good un tewmorrow for Spalding's haysel, I kinder rackun."

" Look well over the water tew."

" Yiss. Good-night, Cady."

" Good-night, Scarlett. See yew at his'n tewmorrow."

And so the days passed and wore themselves into years ; days providing another opportunity of getting ready for the new beginning. And as the years grew so grew the small infirmities into greater, so that Arnold was amongst those who regularly waited on the doctor's visit to the village. His medicine seemed to do him good. Some hard-hearted sceptics said as how Arnold never would be better while he kept on drinking " thet owd stuff he keep makin' on." But as he grew older so he became more and more reminiscent. His school-days at Yoxford. How he left home as a young man and travelled into the foreign parts of Leicestershire ; but he couldn't settle there and soon came home again. How he " larned a bit o' vettin' " with his uncle, and how he worked on this farm and that, and how he

" druv the maale caart," and how he watched that thunder clap knock the corner off the old church. " Standing oova thare, he wur, thet coomed down like a shot out o' my gun."

" But he wur feelin' right queer, thet he wur," and yet people didn't believe him. Sometimes he would not leave his bed for days, and one of his women neighbours would go in and do the best she could for him. And, in due time, as to all men, the last morning came, and it was as though it was that for which he had been preparing all his life—" gettin' ready fur the mornin' " ; the morning to which there would be no night !

And by this natural means came the long talked of, long looked for by some, dispersal of his things. The men in white aprons came and listed the contents of the old home ; bills were put up in the little windows, and another festival day was allotted to the village—an auction !

They held the sale in the front garden, the auctioneer perched up on the top of a large kitchen table on which was placed his chair and table. Indifferent porters brought out the things as best they could, as each lot was called, and the bidding went briskly from the people gathered round the auctioneer's dais. Mrs. Stollery ran up Mrs. Barham for a little table. A stranger bid for the table in three parts. A dealer set his face towards the little bit of silver and the coffin stool without a top, and the old hake which had lain in the yard for so long. Another dealer secured the Paisley shawl, and some of the pictures. But the one priceless old bit, the refectory table, as old as furniture, did not appear, for that had already gone to satisfy the cupidity or covetousness of a new owner.

It was a cloudless lovely day in summer when the dispersal took place ; when the old women hoped to add a few more things to their collection. This bathful of odds and ends ; this trayful of things ; some of his old sheets or well-worn mats. So busy and occupied were they that they had no time to watch the fleas leaping about in the sun from the bedding dropped just outside the front door ; and perhaps, for their peace of mind, it was as well. But was he there on the outskirts of that possessive little company? Did he " whooly laugh tew hisself " as each lot was put up, and successively knocked down to new owners? His glasses that he used to ring when he was showing things to people who called ; his nice little lustre jugs ; his old pudding plate (orange-skin Wedgwood)—" thet hed held many a good owd pudden in its time. Funny wornt it how they scrabbed and scrambled after un " —but he hadn't any use fur them kinder things now ; he wur glad someun thowt suffen o' them. He called tew mind the time he give a few coppers for that at that auction, brought 'em same place as he browt the chairs. But wud yew believe it, they must ha' poured his wine and stout down the drain— what a waste that wur, tew be sure !

And before darkness fell that same day, his own peculiar collection of things that made his home and him, were dispersed—gone like a morning mist, and over the door of the deserted cottage might have been written,—

" Empty vessel, garment cast ! "

JOE BROOM'S SHOP

An old lady went to the stores to buy candles, and was astonished to find that owing to the Spanish-American war " candles was riz."

" Get along ! " she indignantly exclaimed. " Don't tell me they fights by candlelight."

A Cotswold Village—J. ARTHUR GIBBS.

JOE BROOM kept our one and only shop, on the bit of rising ground in the Street as you go to the churchyard gate. He was a born shopkeeper of the line of packmen, higglers and hucksters, and his shop was as great an institution as the church, chapel or pub. Indeed it may be said to have been an almost perfect illustration of that theory of evolution preached by Mr. Darwin about this time.

Joe first began business by peddling things from village to village by means of a little red cart drawn by two dogs ; one Ben a trained and useful thief, the other Susie a more sedate and respectable companion. With this travelling store he made the rounds ; a bit of haberdashery, a bit of Staffordshire pottery, maybe John Wesley preaching under a Gothic arch, yet the two attendant black-haired cherubs do appear a bit fatigued. Or maybe, a pair of dairymaids, Dutch doll-like figures, eternally milking. Or a pair of hounds couchant ; or spaniels statant regardant ! All hidden in one of those capacious baskets or pedders to tempt the eyes of the " wimmen " and those fair-haired, blue-eyed " mawthers," and the money out of their purses ; aided by a bit of consummate salesmanship. Later the equipage was exchanged for a " hoss " and cart, and the catalogue of goods extended. While later still, this equipage grew into the village shop, with its bulging, square-paned windows, and thatched roof.

Here was accumulated and grew, huge stocks of almost

anything that the unsophisticated wants of the local villagers required. An early and rustic edition of Mr. William Whiteley. Tea, brown and white sugar (foot, yellow crystals, demerara, powder-sugar), treacle (drat it ! that hed a nasty habit o' sueing out of the cask), tallow candles, matches, spice, cheese, horn lanterns, rope, boots, spectacles (alias barnacles), straw and felt hats, mixed with soap and oil, and glistering slabs from the salt works at Southwold. The stock was piled in boxes, tumbled on the floor, hung from the low ceiling on all kinds of rusty hooks and spikes, and found its way into the brick-floored, cool cellar below, and into an adjoining cottage which had to be taken for a storehouse, as the business and the stock in trade increased.

Bits of drapery and napery. It was funny to see his horny hands trying to manipulate a few yards of best calico or print, and snipping it off with those gargantuan scissors. And now much funnier to see yards of coloured ribbons sticking to those same hands, wrapping them up—in flaming reds and blues, bright yellows or the most pungent of purples. " I'll rowll thet up, Mister Broom," came as a welcome relief to an irksome duty.

The counters ran round three sides of the shop, with a little smooth wicket gate to act as a flexible link 'twixt vendor and purchaser. The floor was a mixture of stone and wood ; wide old planchers and smooth slabs where the wear came. And if you were lucky, you might get a seat on one or other of those two stools, with their splayed tapering legs, and stretchers worn by many a " grut owd bute." While over all and through all was that fragrance which pervades merchandise in the mass and a country store in particular, which made shopping a sheer delight, and waiting—well, not irksome !

But then there was the character and peculiarities of Joe Broom ; for he held both in high degree. Of average height ; slim, one might almost add thin, with a long hairy fringe that grew from ear to ear, under the

Suffolk Chairs by Daniel and Richard Day of Mendlesham
Photo by courtesy of E.A. Daily Times

Suffolk Chairs, ordinary type

chin but not over it. A pair of quick, beady eyes set above an aquiline nose and the complexion of an apple with skin as smooth. A humorous and twitchy mouth and a pointed chin that seemed almost to make acquaintance with the end of the nose. A high-pitched sing-song voice, not peculiar to Broom, however, and shared by many of his customers, and a most engaging and disarming chuckle. A joke for everyone, even those who owed a bit, he presided over his store with hilarity. And if you'd been waiting rather a long time you might have had a lump of toffee pushed unceremoniously into your mouth with a " stick thet in yar gob, Bob."

The boys and girls didn't always know how to take him, sent as they were on mid-week errands to supply occasional wants, with their lidded wicker-work baskets, or shining tin canisters. He would pop out from the parlour, through the doorway set amid those funny little ill-fitting drawers and shelves, that lined the shop walls, on the ringing of the door bell, that kept on ringing even when the door was closed. More often than not he would appear not to notice the two-feet-six or so of humanity that stood on the other side of the counter, and drum his fingers on the counter top in a curiously clever manipulation of knuckles and finger tips. Then he would bend down until his laughing face was level with his hands, and with the greatest surprise enquire what possibly could be required.

" Wull yew give me a punnarth o' winegar, plaise ? "

" Wall, there bor," would be the pathetic reply, " goo yew home and tell yare mawther all my winegar ha' gone sour ! "

Or, " Can I hev a cow-cumber, plaise ? "

" I han't got one in the place, for all mine are bull-cumbers, this week ! "

And so on, until they agreed among themselves that he was a regular caution !

Yet he was an enterprising and alert merchant as his

career would suggest. For instance, he was the first to have paraffin lamps in his shop, and stocks of oil to supply their wicks; a great advance on the old colza variety and perfectly dazzling as compared with the rushlights or the tallow dips. And was he not responsible for that great festival, a veritable feast of Joe Broom, the Whit-Monday stall? Conceived and carried out as a consummate piece of advertising to coincide with, and cater for, the wants of the chapel goers on their great Whit-Monday meetings and tea.

The stall was erected just outside the shop, at daybreak, on this first real holiday of the year. Relations and friends would assist at its making, and the whole village would rise to the occasion, not forgetting the children. The gals in their clean pinafores and straw hats, gay with flowers; the boys in their patched and descended clothes. Broom's stall; here was something to romp about, something to get right round, something to " garp " at with the most mouth-watering effects. Here they were—sweets, peppermints, bull's eyes, sugar-pigs, toffee apples, gingerbread dots, little cakes made to the shape of all kinds of animals; tops, hoops, dolls, ribbons, Noah's ark, and a model of Middleton mill, made into a loaf of bread baked from Middleton flour, baked in a Middleton oven and destined for Middleton stomachs! What more could you want? Certainly there was nothing finer to be had for miles around; the Whit-Monday tea at the chapel; the Whit-Monday stall at Broom's at the spring of the year.

But Joseph has another claim to immortality besides his shop and his Whit-tide stall, in the shape of a little home-made book, which he kept, made entirely for his own delectation and pleasure. Some six inches by three, it is sewn together with wax thread, probably borrowed from Sam Selfe the cobbler, the pages pencil-lined and written in ink with a laboured, youthful hand.

Here apart from and above his business he kept a record
of the little domestic affairs of his village and time.

Here are recorded, amidst a few accounts, the state
of the weather ; the births, marriages and deaths, a list
of his relations, the accidents, ending up with a few
grand totals.

In September 1837 Joe Broom had goods in hand £40.
Debts in the book £oo. o. o. ; whilst by September 5th,
1843, the debts " on, the slate or on the books " ran to
three figures, now put in cipher, and the laconic remark
" Good " is added. The business was growing !

Then comes the weather. " In 1832, February was
so very dry, scarcely a drop of rain fell."

In 1833 February was very wet, it rained every day
little or much. In 1834 January was so very mild that
turnips were in bloom in many places, and gooseberries
on the bushes as big as peas, but a frost in February
nipt them off ; whilst in the latter part of that month
and the beginning of March the fruit trees were in full
bloom, and all the spring quarter was very hot and dry.
June 21st is recorded as very hot and the wheat harvest
began on the incredibly early date for Suffolk of July 18th ;
ending on August 7th, which was also very hot. The
heat continued all through September into mid-October,
when it set in very cold, until on the 24th there was a
frost. Mildness, however, characterised the season until
December 21st.

1835. Began with favourable weather, with very
little snow in January. February began with slight
frosts, the latter part and the beginning of March very
cold and windy, with rain and sleet. April began cold,
then warm and so it continued till wheat harvest which
began on July 30th.

1841. The weather was favourable till April which
was very hot and dry. May, June and July changeable.
Harvest began on August 6th.

The marriages are set out in the prescribed formula ;

laboriously repeating itself for each occasion,—" Mary
Borrett was married to John Tovell at Middleton by the
Rev. Mr. Packard on April 10th, 1833 " ; until we find
the Rev. Mr. Packard himself fell to the wiles of Miss
Tabitha Devereaux, and he is duly recorded.

The births are punctually noted, with especial reference
to relations, and that peculiar feature, the uncanny hour
at which they take place,—" Mary Wigg was born at
3 o'clock in the morning, it was a Friday."

As to deaths, those outside the parish are not counted,
even the case of such as Jamey Hunt, who died at the
asylum.   One must have died at home to be included ;
however, you might be included in the burials, which was
some consolation.   Neither were stillborns reckoned,
though there is a reference to " No name Bedwell."
And those regrettable lapses to which flesh is heir are
adroitly passed over by the following,—" William
Goddard was called Chambers " !   Accidents, though
labelled plural, are in the singular, to wit,—" George
Brabner's leg broken January 12th, 1835 "—cause
unknown.

And then we have that concise summary, which is not
without interest,—

In 1829 there were 12 Births, 1 Death, 1 Burial.

1830	13	9	10	
1831	20	12	11	
1832	15	11	12	5 Married.
1833	20	10	9	9
1834	14	15	15	3

Running through the whole record are such names as
Ellsworthy, Barley, Chambers, Foulsham, Blofield,
Woolnough, Larter, Goddard, Wigg, Pipe, Free, Catch-
pole.   With Christian names of Azor, Alma, Zippiah,
Louisa (spelt Loezer), Pharaoh, Noah, Mahala.   While
scrawled on the covering leaf, a whole page to itself,
" William the Fourth was crowned September 8th,
1831."

Broom also aspired to poetry and was wont to carry on a rhyming correspondence with a traveller, who replied in like strain. Here is a sample of the cross-current,—

> On July 9, 'twixt morn and noon,
> Jude hopes to see his old friend Broom,
> To feel his pulse and grasp his hand,
> Then at his counter take his stand ;
> The various samples he can show,
> In prices high and prices low,
> From Royal silk to peasant jute ;
> The value prime none can dispute.
> Blankets and flannels fine and stout,
> Such goods will make the people shout.
> Look out friend Joe, straight forward look,
> And when Jude comes just fill his book.
>
> Dear Mr. Jude, your old friend Joe,
> Fears as you come you'll have to go.
> From Royal silk to peasant jute,
> No doubt all parties you can suit ;
> Your winceys, flannels, blankets all
> Would please the great as well as small ;
>
> You may have " lines " both good and bad,
> To try them all I should be glad.
> I fear your book you cannot fill,
> I'm short of money in the till ;
> So drive on quick and make haste home,
> You won't do much with old
>
> > Joe Broom.

Of course Broom had his favourites (who hasn't ?) in the way of customers. And perhaps the chief of these was Miss Martha Fellowes, who lived in that neat little stuccoed villa of a house with the graceful porticoed porch supported by those slender fluted pillars, as you turn towards the Moor just after leaving the Carnser. A funny little dark-featured woman with a bent back that gave her an almost deformed appearance. Her dark features suggested something of the wise-woman,

which suggestion was added to by her expert ability to
" tell " the cups of her visitors at afternoon tea—an
occupation she loved. Her eyes would sparkle as she
handled, delicately, Mrs. Hamilton's cup. The parson's
wife usually came on Thursdays, her flat black-straw
hat tied under her plump chin with a wisp of silk.
Always talking of the Rector ; and how she thought
Martha and she should go in for a donkey apiece—they
could then go to Yoxford shopping. But donkeys had
such a bad habit of stopping dead—" quite dead, my
dear "—when you had an excellent opportunity of
showing your horsemanship, or your agility. And
Martha would reply, with the faintest twinkle, that she
could see two mokes—yes two—and there was a ditch
and a prickly hedge. " Can't you see them, dear Mrs.
Hamilton ? There they are, and that really does look
like you in the ditch, doesn't it ? I think we had better
keep to Broom, after all ! " Yet she was as agile as a
leveret, with a quick step that developed into a run.
She could come downstairs at seventy, as quickly and as
agile as a girl of twenty, with a gliding motion that
hardly suggested stairs and feet but rather the trippings
of a fairy.

Rumour had it that she came of the peerage, and
rumour had it too, that on the corners of her sheets and
linen were to be found neat little crowns worked in red
cotton with a fine and noble stitch.

She used to enter Broom's shop almost apologetically,
certainly kiender-sidous (sideways), and would make
her purchases with as fine a discrimination as she knew
how. A little of this, a little of that, until there was
quite an array of little packets on the counter, done up
mostly in those cone-shaped bags, which in due time
she would transfer to her lidded basket en route to her
pantry. Broom was a great radical, but like all radicals,
he had a sneaking regard for the landed gentry though
wild horses wouldn't have dragged such an admission

from him, and he had a great regard for Martha
Fellowes. They would fall to mardling about this and
that, and if so be that he knew of a deserving case which
needed a little timely charity he would acquaint Martha
of the fact. He knew her weaknesses and how she had
parted with one of her few five pound notes to that
charlatan of an old sailor who pitched such a yarn of
woe when he knocked at her back door. And how she
let another go to the enterprising blacksmith who had
produced a patent drill and wanted to get it on the
market. Years he'd been on that old contraption, and
all he wanted was a little money to finish it off. Pay
her back, that he would, but of course he never did,
because he never got so much as five pounds out of the
blamed thing !

Martha Fellowes was a religious enough church-goer
and worshipper, yet strange to tell had more than one
God. There was the one she worshipped in the church
under the direction of our parson, and the one she
worshipped at home in the person of her dear cousin
the poet. His slightest words she regarded as having
been spoken on Sinai, while his printed volume was as
an extension of the ancient Prophets. Abel was
spoken of, thought of, dreamt of, as with bated breath
and the utmost adoration. But then, after all, she
was only half of this earth ; her feet none too firmly
placed ; which might account for her numerous falls, or
bouncings ; while her head was of the mist that wraps
itself about our willow tops !

Another of Broom's customers, though not in the
running of favourites, was old Baker Free. Mechanically
minded, born before his time, he dabbled in disused
railway carriages and any old steam engine that, with a
fire in its belly, could still possibly take the road. He
used to come in with grimy hands, his face (save for two
twinkling dark eyes) almost hidden by a huge wild
beard, for a little oil or tow, or maybe a rope.

You could hear his old fire eaters a-puffing along our quiet roads, making such a smoke as never was, and spluttering as though they would " bust tharesalves " ! Usually they got stuck on that nasty little rise, just as you come up from the level bit by Joe King's corner, and then there'd be a rare to-do. Shoutings, mixed up with the shriek of escaping steam, with two of his boys standing at the ready with an old sleeper, with which to scotch up the wheels ; the ancient machine would rise inch by inch to the very top. But the greatest indignity of all, was when Baker had to get a team of horses from Rackford farm to get the duzzy thing to move even an inch. And when he did eventually get it home, he broke it up in sheer desperation. But he rarely loved those funny old funnels and a drop of that black smoke gave him a fine appetite.

And then there was Sarah Butcher, who used to come to him for bars and bars of soap, added to her groceries, all of which she would wheel home in one of those ancient prams, with thick wooden wheels that used to grate finely over the gritty roads. She had a rare old clack, had Sarah, and an outsider, not knowing the peculiarities, would have concluded that a regular row was going on 'twixt she and Broom, whereas nothing was further from the truth. They would be just running over old experiences and times. For example, before Sarah had married Noah she had spent a few years in London as a cook, and she was never loath to tell Broom of the wonders of such an experience ; as indeed, with Noah, whom she was apt to discount as never having been out of the parish. This was the Noah who was gardener to the parson and superintendent at the chapel Sunday school and who administered large cuffs to unruly boys in sermon time ! A genial cheery soul whose smacks were given with smiles !

Sarah's main task in life, after having reared a family in the most exemplary manner—they had all gone into

the old perambulator in turn—was to take in washing.
This used to arrive in great hampers, conveyed by the
coachman from the Hall ; and as the week wore through
stacks of billowy white clothes would strew her rooms,
before being ironed with those old box and smoothing
irons and folded and repacked in the hampers.

Sarah was a fine piece of a woman, not much shaped
perhaps ; wide at the base, slowing narrowing towards
the head ; which head, when out, was surmounted by a
black, round straw hat which gave her an almost churn-
like appearance. But my heart ! she could talk, that she
could ; in which direction she made up for any deficien-
cies in her pleasant-faced smiling but over-shadowed
husband. And if she could talk, so also could she work,
and she made those " darters " of hers work too, who
assisted her in the laundering, and a little in the talking !

And so they would come, with their varying needs as
indeed they varied in character and appearance. The
Prophet's wife, hobbling on her poor old feet, to collect
a bottle of medicine left in this central depot for callers.
" Owd Polly Wincent, who ullus axed Broom for
suffen he hadn't gort ; the owd worrit—I rackun she
did it a purpose." The new maid at the Rectory for a
" dwile " with which to wash the floors. Nan Baggot
for some grey-powders for father ; and the boy John
for a Jew's harp or " haff a yard o' lastic, plaize."
Besides the regular callers on Thursdays or Fridays for
scraps or chitterlings, if so be that a pig had gone the
way of pigs that week ; or a little bit o' drippin' !

Or uncle Frank would come in for a new flashing
hook or maybe a scythe, for Broom kept such things and
always the best, bought from those old edge tool makers
over at Leiston. You could always tell where uncle
Frank lived, for he used to hang his scythe in the apple
tree and there it stuck all the winter, just to get it into
trim for the haysel. Or perhaps it was a stone he
wanted because his " owd un hed gort brooke ! "

But the end, fitting, perhaps, though tragic, came to Broom's shop, if it came not to Broom himself. One night the word went round, heads were thrust out into the darkness, and, there was our church spire thrown up like a ghost against the night, by a glow that was Broom's shop going up in flames. Willing helpers were soon astir, for in common with man and the beasts, fire is a fearful elemental thing; to be dreaded and fought. They dragged off the burning thatch with the dragging hooks, kept at the church for this purpose. They even brought the old hand-manual from Yoxford under its captain—Ben Rouse—imperturbable Ben, who drove the horses into a fine lather and all but winded them. They ran the hose into the ditch by the Carnser, and five men aside seized the rail, and pumped and pumped, as though they were in the harvest field; while a chain of men and boys was soon at work with the old leather buckets. That old nozzle threw a mighty fine little jet into the flames; but there, what was the good? It was like a doctor at a death-bed; there to acquiesce with the inevitable and sign the certificate. And it was so with Ben, as he took off his helmet and wiped the grime and sweat from his forehead and exclaimed " Whew." That " Whew " was the sign they might pack up and " goo whome; for there worn't no manner o' use o' them staying there and garping at thet owd ruin ! "

THE CENTENARIAN

Had I been one of her relations, and as well enabled as most of them be, I would have erected a monument for her—thus designed. A fair tree should have been erected, the said lady and her husband lying at the bottom or root thereof; the heir of the family should have ascended both the middle and top bough thereof. On the right hand thereof her younger sons, on the left her daughters should, as so many boughs, be spread forth. Her grandchildren should have their names inscribed on the branches of those boughs; the great-grandchildren on the twigs of those branches; the great-great-grandchildren on the leaves of those twigs. Such as survived her death should be done in a lively green, the rest (as blasted) in a pale and yellow fading colour.

FULLER.

LENGTH of days is very common in Suffolk, and Centenarians are numerous, for as the worthy Fuller observes,—" The air thereof generally is sweet and by the best physicians esteemed the best in England." Add to this the static nature of the countryside, its peaceful avocations, its almost withdrawal from the " madding " world, and you have much of the cause. Persons of extreme age can tell of but little change from the days of their youth; change, perhaps, in customs and manners, but little change in the village and its appearance. The old church, water supply, sanitation— or the absence of it—even the village street, just the same as when they first knew it and went to shop for mother, or to scare crows for old farmer Winter at the Hawthorns. And after all, the " tenements, messuages and pightles " are still handed on at the old-time Michaelmas (Oct. 11th), albeit now by Land Registry rather than the sealed vellum manuscripts, drawn up in the best penmanship and laboriously signed, Samuel Selfe, his mark ! New owners but old landmarks !

Harriet Marjoram was a magnificent specimen of a woman to the very end of her long life. Seated in the wooden armchair or walking down the village street to shop or chapel, or pottering about her own cottage; a marvel of upstanding and height at such an advanced age. Neatly dressed, in ancient clothes, that were continuously but finely repaired, complete with cap or bonnet, she was a marvel of economical living. She came out of the years when things were prized and cared for, when some things were extremely expensive and scarce; and all of this had left a mark on her outlook and practice of domestic economy. Needlecraft, in her young days, was not merely a refinement of the high schools, but the everyday accomplishment of the home, together with so much else that became the housewife and the mother. She wore her clothes until they took on that greeny hue with which Nature adorns age whether of an old wall or a life, partly because they were old and therefore had associations with the past, but chiefly because that was her careful way of life. In her young days a man bought a suit of clothes in his youth to last him for the rest of his life, and the same thing applied to the women. In her case, however, most of her wardrobe had been handed on from other owners and she was successful in putting the lie to the old saying that clothes of the dead, when given away, never wore well.

She was widowed long years by an accident in the harvest-field; a happening not uncommon at such a season of the year. On this occasion it was runaway horses; but always it was a cause for thankfulness if the harvest passed without incident of either a fatality or permanent injury. His old broad-brimmed hat with its greasy band hung from behind her door, while his sad, serious shadow of a face looked down from an enlargement on the wall of her little room, as though waiting patiently for that other harvest which would bring them together again. He must have been a comparatively young man when he went, but he looked strangely old and a trifle tired. The ancient House of Marjoram was well known about here, for it was only at Yoxford that a poetic sign over the door of one, spoke, or sung, as follows,—

> James Majouram does live here,
> He sweeps the chimineys far and near ;
> If your chiminey get on fire,
> He'll put it out at your desire.
> If, ladies and gentlemen, you will call,
> He'll try and wait upon you all !

But, of course, they didn't so desire, especially if they had just given it a charge of gunpowder to clear it out !

With a large family, fifteen to be exact, she faced life with courage and a stoic fortitude, and launched all these her children on the world to be a credit to herself and her county. Policemen, soldiers, or in " sarvice," they did well and ever looked back to their home and their mother with gratefulness and thanks.

But she was a " rum 'un " to live with in her old age ; in fact, it couldn't be done even by daughters. After having brought up a family of your own, and to have grandchildren yourself, it is a bit trying at seventy to be scolded by an irate parent of ninety odd about opening " they winders," or for using more than one match a day—one to light the fire, all other lights to be had by spills—or, if you should accidentally break an already cracked pie-pan, for " hurling the potsherds abroad " when, perchance, they might have been " shut " together for further service. After all there are limits of endurance as there are extremities of economics !

Perhaps it was but natural that she should live in the past, for she had seen great changes in the conduct of life, changes as revolutionary and as far reaching as it was possible for one life to experience. Out of one age, the England of Elizabeth, into the era of the motor car. It was a different matter being a farmer's boy, and sowing and reaping in her young days, to what it was when she sat in her chair and reflected on those who had gone. When her husband went out in the morning at daybreak, with his wickle-poke full of hard home-made bread and hard cheese, and a stone bottle full of home-brewed beer, he went to take his place amongst the wielders of the scythe, whose music was not merely in the rhythm of the mowing and the swish of the blade, but also in the whetting of the scythe.

> Hark ! where the sweeping scythes now rips along :
> Each sturdy mower, emulous and strong,
> Whose writhing form meridian heat defies,
> Bends o'er his work, and every sinew tries ;
> Prostrates the waving treasures at his feet,
> But spares the rising clover, short and sweet.

And it was the same with ploughing and sowing. Up and down the fields, behind the straining horses, day in and day out, to be followed by the harrow and then the seed lip, with again a musical motion of left and right as the seed was broadcast. Or perhaps the seed was dibbled in by an expert, followed close up by young children who would drop in one or two kernels, just the right amount and with great dexterity and speed. But nowadays, " bless 'ee, it's all done in a few many days by a little fulla who hardly gits 'is butes dutty. My haart, thet's a rum 'un, thet thet is. Thet wur rare backaachin' wurk when my poor husband wrought, thet et wur ! It's the same at haysel an' harvest—they owd machines cum an scrab away, end afore yew ken say ' cock farden ' they'm a done, an' it's back in the stackyerd. I mind when we used tew gew a glanin'— the bell 'ud ring from the owd church at eight a-clock, an' we'd be off ; an' we used tew git enow wittals fur a quarter. Rouse at the Mill used tew grind it for us. And then we'd hev a rale good time at the Horkey ; owd John 'ud be Lord an' my husband Lady, and ther'd be a rare frolic."

And then the changes in everyday life, though love

and courting, marriage and death are much the same as ever. The babes in her young days were kept in the dark, lest the light should affect their eyes, while now, " they're tunned abroad as soon as they're born." " But there, we had all kinds o' quare thowts then. We didn't think it nohow right to weigh 'em, fur if we did they udn't thrive ; like a watched kettle I kinder rackun. But then a child 'ud never thrive well until it wor named, fur Christenin' wur a rare cure fur sickness. And it worn't good fur children tew lie on bones—laps they meant—and I doan't fare tew think they was fur wrong. And when they left their mother's bedroom fur the first time they must ullus gew upstairs afore they gew down, else they wudn't git on in the warld. But bless 'ee, most o' places round hare hadn't gort any more ' ups ' so we used tew git oova thet by steppin' on tew a chair and holding the babe up in our arms. Then folks as aready gort a dale of childrin, coulna bear tew see an empty cradle rocked in their house. If they see one o' they little uns a doin' sich a thing, they'd stop 'em right quick. As fur cats, they said they 'ud suck the breath out o' a babe's body. But if a mother giv' away all her babe's clothes, or the cradle, thinkin' as how she hed finished wi' thet sort o' thing, she'd sure tew hev another babe afore long."

" Then in my young days it wor rare fur the children tew gew away, but now there's no accounting wher they'll be as sune as they leave schule. We used tew marry one another until the whool village wur divided atween two or three families. But thet aint accounted roight tew-day; but, there, I never see'd anything amiss in thet ; though I must say as how most villages had their idiots. But I hev heerd as how madness hasn't bin whooly stamped out, enen in Lunnon ! "

And then how superstitious they were when she was young, for witches had hardly died when she was a girl. As near to her birth as 1825 they had " swum " an old man in the " Grimmer "—a large pond on the green—at Wickham Skeith for the supposed practise of evil influence on a woman. She could remember old Nan Sprunt who lived up by Title, who had as bad a name as ever woman failed to merit.

" One day, when I wur a churning at the Pack Way farm, who should cum tew the backus door, but owd Nan. ' Could she hev sum butter? ' Missus wur riled about suffin and sent her a gooin'. Dew yew think we could git any butter arter thet in thet duzzy owd churn —no, we couldna. Thet oudn't come nohow ; it only slumped from side tew side, and when we looked in thar warn't nornt but milk. All at once Missus got thet agitated she sed she rackuned owd Nan hed bewitched it, so she up wi the box iron, made it thet red hot an' swep it in the churn. Thet whooly sizzled, thet thet did, I ken tell ee, an' the butter cum, amost at once, though a bit oily like. Dew yew know thet owd Nan cum round agin the vary nixt morning, but she hed an awful bad heel—thet wur barnt ! "

" Then we used tew grow they owd Jupiter's Beards on the thetch tew keep away devils and sich like ; but they doan't fare tew want them these days wi' tiles and slaates."

She could recall too, the old wart curers ; how they always carefully asked the number of the warts, and then said no more, but somehow the warts disappeared. And how they were not above passing naked children through a cleft ash tree, at sunrise, with its head towards the rising sun, to cure hernia, or " bussen-belly " as it was called.

And sometimes, if you had gone in unawares, you might have caught her putting the poker cross-wise against the grate, to make the dull fire burn a bit brighter. Her mother had done that years before her time and it was always effective.

And, of course, there was a whole rigmarole about the

Aged five, inclined to cry . . . in her best go-to-chapel frock and boots, holding an orange ; and " whooly " frightened of the travelling photographer as he pops his head under the black cloth ! Taken in Bell Yard, Middleton, 1862

You can often pick up a bit of news here

Bees. They had to be " told " of a death, and a piece of mourning tied to the old bee skep. And they wouldn't thrive if there was contention in the house ; while if you harboured a stray swarm in your garden, it would only bring you trouble.

And everyone was mightily afraid of ghosts ; they seemed to be in most large houses, and most folks had had some experience of them. Strange moving figures or lights ; presages of evil to come And if you were born in the " Chime-hours "—8, 12, 4—you were gifted with second sight ; whilst if at other hours then you were free of ghosts and had no need to fear.

To the last, Harriet preferred to do her own bit of washing and cooking, and was not unequal to turning the bit of fruit from her garden bushes into a bottle of wine, of which she was proud to offer you a glass should you pay her a visit. How fine she looked as she stood up to reach down the bottle from the top shelf of the corner cupboard ! And her hands were steady as she poured out a glass of Cowslip or Rhubarb or Elder.

The afternoon would find her in her old wooden chair, upright but resting, with her feet on the home-made rug of cloth pieces, made when she was a young woman. No, not dozing, for that might rob her of her night's rest and find her lying awake, listening for sounds in the so quiet night. But just reflecting on old ways, old days, old faces, through all the long and quiet years. Of the old farmer who had a penchant for having his cows and bullocks washed before they went into the byres, and his pigs likewise, as he preferred clean animals to dirty. Of the brewings and the bakings and her old pattens with which she used to click over the stones. How they used to bury the small-pox cases by lantern light in the churchyard and how often the parson was so scared he'd read the service from the church porch. Of how one or two venturesome ones from the village went up to London to see the Great Exhibition,

H

and sailed from Slaughden Quay in the "Amity" (Capt. J. Dance) making their way to Fennings Wharf, London Bridge. And how folks would think "nawthing" of walking to Ipswich and back, though they might get a lift in one of those lumbering owd waggons, that plied along the turnpike. Perhaps, one of old Sam Noller's waggons, with a horn lantern hung up on the tilt, that made the journey from London to Yoxford.

· And then she would have her bit of tea ; put a wedge under the old black kettle and make it boil ; soak her rusk in the tea or mumble a little bread and butter. Then do a bit of mending ; somehow there had been rents to sew up all her life long ; her old clothes were a visible proof of that ; while her stockings—as green as her outer clothes—were new footed and new legged, until not much of the original remained. And then off to bed, lighting herself up those crooked steep little stairs with an old metal candlestick, much older even than herself, and which she would recall used to hold those old tallow candles that had an awkward knack of "snasting" every few minutes and so needed constant attention. And she might even admit that these new "twelveses" were a great improvement on the old, and will burn themselves out without the least attention, always with an eye on the candle-thief, to say nothing of the matches—"they funny owd sulphur things thet used tew whooly smell." And then up betides, to start the daily round again, with its meals and its mendings.

And Sunday would find her making her stately way along the Street, across the green, to the square-faced chapel, that was just about her own age. Twice a day, afternoon and evening, she would be there in her same old pew ; her face agleam, her quavering voice joining in the hymns, following the singers.

" Ah, I hev sat under a mort o' preachers in my toime, thet I hev. They used tew coom in thair traps and put thaire hosses up at the Bell ; but now they cumes in they owd fly abouts, but thare sarmons arn't nohows better ! They used tew stick tew the Wud and praiche fur they hour tewgither, an' I cud a gone on listening fur ullus. And they used tew pray rare long prayers in them days, and folks ud kip on saying ' Amen ' and ' Glory ' and some 'ud even start singing a hymn right in the middle. I mind when owd Charlie Chambers had been a going for about a score a minutes, he cawt cramp, and shruck out so thet we wundered what hed happened. Poor owd Aunt Mahala hed a lovely death, thet she did, she slipped away when owd Billy Rouse wur a wrastlin', and they dina know as she wur stiff until he'd finished haff an hour arterwards !

" But thare, they're awl gone,—Aunt Mahala, uncle Frank, cousin John, Naomi, Nobbler Brown, Zipporah, I can see 'em all, bless 'em ; and I fare tew be the only one left. No aunts, no uncles, no grandfather, no grandmother, no nawthing ! "

And she, Harriet Marjoram, who saw the light as Victoria saw the throne of England, lived to her one hundredth birthday ; saw the cake with its array of candles—candles had played a great part in her life—received the Royal greetings, had about her her sons and daughters—many of them now old men and women—then lighted her way to bed with that same antique steel candlestick, to the old four-poster, with its shadows, its curtains of red moreen, and its peculiar enticements of dreams and long, long memories. Had it not been her first job on rising each day to knock out the doke left by her body in the bed, lest some spell should be woven about her ?

But the excitement was too great, and she, who appeared as though she might go on for ever, must of necessity pass to the quiet acre, where her husband had lain so long ; to the faded company of the old photograph, who once stood out so clear against the sun, and in which she formed a youthful part.

They gathered round her bed ; there could hardly be sadness ; her old shrunken form propped up by pillows, her shrivelled, tenuous hands plucking at the coverlet, her lace night-cap holding in place the few remaining fragments of a once dark and glossy head, and still her eyes took note, still was her carefulness manifest,— " Yew'll find 'em in thet owd chest yonder." Things gathered and preserved years agone now ; not new, but acquired during the association of others in like state to herself now. But all spotlessly clean, smelling of lavender, carefully washed and ironed and goffered. White night-dress, white gloves, white stockings, and the daintiest of white caps, prepared with meticulous care for this great occasion, this long-deferred burying, or should we not rather say, this new marriage ?

THE TWO SQUIRES

Mr. Knightley's air is so remarkably good that it is not fair to compare Mr. Martin with him. You might not see one in a hundred, with gentleman so plainly written as in Mr. Knightley. But he is not the only gentleman you have been lately used to. What say you to Mr. Weston and Mr. Elton? Compare Mr. Martin with either of them. Compare their manner of carrying themselves; of walking; of speaking; of being silent. You must see the difference.

Emma—JANE AUSTEN.

As we had to go outside the parish for the doctor, so must we also for the Squire, but in this case we have the choice of two, though only one belongs by right to our parish and might therefore be accounted its squire. If for no other reason, however, than a study in contrasts we shall do well to consider both.

Suffolk has reason to be proud of her squires, for to them she owes much; in fact, she is in debt to them to her very tree tops. The charm of the county, its very freedom from spoliation, and its serenity, is largely due to the estates which they have fostered and cared for through so many troublous and unfriendly years. Running about their estates on their beloved chestnuts, wearing immaculate blue coats, white hats and trousers in summer, full of " damns," as, for instance, the one who took the chair at a meeting of the local Bible Society and referred to it as a " damned good Society which ought to be damned well supported." Or masquerading as scarecrows with old ancient clothes that could never be given away or worn out—the envy of all local tramps and the despair of their dames.

The real thing in squires is the result of many generations—not forgetting the law of primogeniture. No amount of wealth can produce them, neither can they be found suddenly in some populous city and transplanted to carry out their functions by virtue of purchase or election. They belong to the old Manors and their Courts, must have their roots in the soil and be the peculiar product of their locality. They do not spring up in a night, neither do they vanish with the morning ; and it will be a sorry day for England if they are ever cast out and their lands removed from them.

Of course they are not without idiosyncrasies or free from imperfections or beyond criticism. We all know, and have heard, of pump chainings, and browbeatings at election times, and petty oppressions and threats. And of those who thought the Church was a Divine institution in which to place his numerous relations in comfortable livings. But we can also recall threats to burn down the " Hall " ; and we must not forget that in many cases it was they who built and maintained the schools, if it cannot be said they had any hand in building the chapels ! And you may rail at them, and recall the escapades of runagate sons, but the fact remains that the perfect man is neither with the Squirearchy nor the proletariat !

First then, the Squire who lives N.E. of our village and whom we consider with only indirect implication as having any overlordship in this parish. He was typical of his class and his day, coming from a long way in the historical line, even from that Lord Mayor of London in the reign of Edward VI. He lies now, with his fathers, in that prison-like vault built within the chapel of the old Lazar Hospital. A grim forbidding place, where slimy mallow, tenuous ivy and elder, wrestle frantically in a vain endeavour to clothe mortality with beauty.

This line had represented the Pocket Borough of a village in Parliament on the strength of a dozen votes until the Reform Bill altered the balance of power. But they had also fought in their country's wars, not forgetting Corunna and that little episode at Waterloo, as indeed they still do fight !

But the Squire of our consideration was a decided bit of curio—as individual as anything Suffolk could produce ; he belonged to the " mawkin " variety. His clothes hung about him—not always with the odour of sanctity, if for instance his long-suffering lady should discover a dead rabbit or a decomposed pheasant in one of his large pockets. His boots, as soon as received from the maker, were hacked by his own hands into a peculiar form of highlows until they resembled mediaeval footwear, while he was always careful that his socks should be boiled to a dirty grey before he would wear them. An old hat, presumably reived from the middle of a field, and a neckerchief that appeared to have done duty as a foot-bandage in the Crimea, went to the making of such a picture of distress that so touched the heart of an innocent stranger as to cause him to offer sixpence to help so distressed a case.

He was the proud owner of two estates. One inland, purchased by his grandfather from the drooping hands of an ancient family—do they not lie in the effulgence of knighthood in that little church hard by the mansion, set deep in the park ? But it was a good stroke of business on the purchaser's part, for he sold sufficient timber off the estate without doing it despite, to pay for the purchase. Evidently some of the old Lord Mayor's blood still lingered in his veins. And the other estate, of many acres, the ownership of which is in constant dispute 'twixt himself and the sea, and as the latter takes the law into its own watery fingers, he stood to lose, slowly but surely.

And he preferred this little patrimony to the former, so he spent most of his time in that picturesque little shooting-box of a residence, built in the best country-house Gothic, which was as snugly furnished as the art of the Squiress could achieve. Covered with thatch, it was a curious bit of architecture, looking for all the world like a doll's house or a china money-box. But it had been added to from time to time, so it ambled and rambled about in a manner sufficient to deceive the casual onlooker, if not the inmates themselves.

The entrance door, surmounted by an arched fanlight, had rustic pillars supporting the portico, which were supplemented by other pillars that held up the thatch as it ran round the semi-circular walls of the west front, and the flat side to the north, about which Maiden's Blush and honeysuckle gambled in riotous profusion during the whole of spring and summer.

Inside, the door opened into a small hall, at the back of which were the stairs of polished black oak, uncarpeted, and when they were washed it was a fresh pail of water to two stairs ! Their neatly turned balusters went up to a half-landing and then turned east and west to the rooms above. East to the servants' quarters ; west to the better bedrooms.

Staircases, even the smallest, have a fascination of their own and this was no exception, with its hand-smooth rail running up like a thread from the newel post below, and a domed space for a china closet nestling safely under the half-landing.

The rooms on the ground floor were long and low ; lightened by fairly large-paned windows that served to brighten the rather heavy interiors ; panelled walls and beamed ceilings and curtained as they were. Mrs. Squire was as proud of her " chaney " curtains as any farmer's wife on the estate. The rooms were not heavily furnished but contained those comfortable pieces that would be priceless to-day. Fishing rods, guns and telescopes adorned the living room, mixed with a few prints of horses and sporting scenes. Not many books, yet one with pride of place on the Squire's bureau—the one with the cathedral window-like doors— to wit, *Complete Justice*. Upstairs, the wide floor boards seemed to amble along invitingly to a series of low-ceilinged rooms, with worn thresholds. In the case of the east end, to the one small room at the extremity, where, it was alleged, "walked" the ghost of poor Sam Selfe, the drowned sailor, drowned off the Cache Cliff, when he was doing a bit of "running." With his guttering tallow candle in one hand, his red tasseled sailor's cap hanging on the back of his neck, shivering as though just out of the water, he seemed in perpetual concern over something lost that could not be recovered. How he came to be in the Squire's house is not quite clear, but here he was every wane of the moon. And why not ? When the sea was just below the meadow at the end of the lawn, and one day would have the house and its memories within its watery waste ! Perhaps he had something to do with that strange little incident of the stray cannon ball that embedded itself by the manger in the stable one foggy autumn morning shot out of the greyness of the sea, no one knew how or why, and from which of His Majesty's ships.

Outside in the garden, clustering about the house, were numerous outbuildings, providing plenty of covered space. The Laundry, with its washing and drying rooms ; Bakehouse and Brewery, the latter provided with varying degrees of coppers, each with its deep-set furnace-like fire-hole. The dairy and cheese room, and not least an ample amount of stabling. Here could be seen old harness, and brass ornaments for the horses, and a curious collection of vehicles that had belonged to father and grandfather—whiskys, barouches, phaetons, including the cabriolet in which his father used to post to London for the reassembling of Parliament, making for Piccadilly, with a stop for one night at Colchester.

He, as his lady, was a great horseman, and the stable door was covered with shoes, duly inscribed with attainments at gallops for miles around. Such was his passion that if he got wind of a donkey race on the sands to mark some festive occasion, he could be relied upon to enter his runner from amongst the mokes who found a living in the gardens. His passion, too, led him to have a circular covered way erected in the grounds of the Shrubbery, around which he could canter to his heart's content, in all weathers.

But on Sundays you would find his grey hunter tied up to the ancient yew tree, outside the church door, while he, with his house, worshipped.

Life for him was marked by certain cardinal numbers in the calendar, such as the 12th, 1st, etc., and he liked nothing better than, dressed in his oldest scarecrow clothes, to go for a day's wild-fowl shooting with Arnold, one of his tenants. The relationship was of equals, and they would start before daybreak. Arnold was a rare practitioner with punt and gun and his soft " Hare they coom, Master ! " was as music to the squire. It was a breathless suspense as to whether they would be out of reach, left, right or slap over head. The art of hiding was as well known to these two as to the birds themselves, while they could sit as squat as an old harnser at the rush-grown bends. In and out of creeks, crawling along the dangerous mud banks, until they could hear the " whee-ou " of widgeons, flash a mallard, empty a few barrels at wild duck or snipe, or outwit the cunning of wild geese. Bess would be sent to bring in the prey, which had often to be retrieved from difficult and dangerous places, but she never failed or harmed the birds, for her mouth was as tender as that of her pups. But she could nohow abide the smell of woodcock and always gave them an extra wide berth ! Then home at long past dark, tired but chuckling ; squire to his port and Arnold to his home-brewed, or maybe, a bottle from the same cellar as that of the squire. The joy of the day was not measured by the size of the bag, but the fine cunning of real sportsmanship which could be retold over pipe and glass.

Another time it would be an evening after the old

Dows that had been " a scrabbing the crops wholesale " ;
but they wanted a deal of shooting, "drat 'em." You
might get a few as they drifted in " tew winnard " ;
while pigeon pie was held in good tidy esteem by both
of them.

The Squire's humour was his own, as when the
immaculate visitor came to stay at the Shrubbery, of
whose appearance the squire took especial note. He
must needs show him round the estate himself and at
once. At speed they crossed the newly ploughed fields,
took short cuts through the thickest brakes, until Savile
Row would have failed to recognise its own creation !

The second Squire, who may be well said to be our
squire proper, was as different to the one just described
as could be found in the county. A man of books and
learning ; of his garden, his Palladian mansion and his
village. His estate just comes within the confines of
our village, by his farms which stretch to the high
ground contiguous to the Moor. A quiet, gentle sort
of creature, fond of antiquities and local links with the
past ; deeply attached to his gentle partner and his
family, he spent his days between his study and the
care of his estate and people. The lawn, in front of the
Hall, stretching to the ha-ha, was always thrown open
in spring to the villagers, in order that they might
gather the cowslips which there grew in abundance.
Cottagers in need were always visited by either himself
or his gentle wife, and presents made of coals or blankets,
soups or bread ; while the clothing of his children were
always dispersed to the growing girls and boys of the
growing cottage homes.

His garden had been well laid out with old red walls ;
and a central clock tower on the stables which tinkled
quietly the hours ; while his shiny little carriage, conveying him or his womenfolk, was always to be seen
plying about the village or to the nearby little township
on shopping bent.

The old house was typical of its day—comfortable almost to spaciousness, complete with picture gallery and the most elaborate of ballrooms, which he added as to well-nigh beggar himself ; yet it had no adequate water supply, and certainly no bathroom. An army of servants must fetch and carry every drop of the precious fluid to all parts of the mansion—handled up from a pump in the stone-flagged abutment to the large kitchen. No mean labour, which was accepted as being part of life and in no way out of the common.

In most respects a typical English squire, related to most other families in the county, witness his shields in the old Saxon-towered church—his boys went into the service of their country. One to win the V.C., another to become an Admiral ; whilst his brother, their uncle, elected to wander in Arabia, live as a Bedouin, not without wistful thoughts of the old village and its fields ; of the old house, its pictures and its associations, and to act as a forerunner of those cryptic, powerful persons who have achieved so much for their country in the cementing of friendship between Arab and English.

The old house lies mouldering to ruin now, and the choice little park is reverting to that primeval bush from which it was fashioned, but the cowslips still blow in the now uncared-for grass of the lawn. But no pony chaise rolls along the grass-grown gravel walks, neither is the Town house required for the London Season or the ballroom for the stately dance. And the village and the community is that much the poorer.

THE DOCTOR

If the medicinal prospectus of the leaves, bark, berries, etc., were thoroughly known, I cannot tell what our countryman could ail for which he might not find a remedy from every hedge, either for sickness or wound.

JOHN EVELYN.

No, Edward Bailey was not merely an " owd hoss doctor " ; that is a complete and utter libel. He had duly served an apprenticeship to a surgeon at Ipswich, for the space of five years—had been bound duly and truly " his master faithfully to serve, his secrets keep, his lawful commands everywhere gladly to do." In return for which and in consideration that he refrained from cards, dice, or the haunting of taverns, his master provided him with sufficient meat, drink, lodgings, washing and mending, and launched him on the world and Suffolk in particular as a doctor.

True, he appeared perfectly at home with dogs and horses, and could tell you what to do with your cow, and " thet thare young cowt " and he might have been a little rough and ready, with little or none of that bedside manner that is such an asset to-day. He showed but little trace of any claim to a classical education, except on the occasion when, walking into the sunlit kitchen parlour of old John Barham,—who was upstairs in bed, on one of his infrequent occasions—he caught the cat on the table taking advantage of the situation with a spread meal, with a wholesome cuff and the remark,—" He didn't think that Nemesis was so near ! " But in reality he was as gentle as the mouth of his owd " dawg " ; always realising that the mouth held a good set of teeth and could bite. His ability as a doctor was considerable, and what he lacked in book learning he made up in horse sense,—no mean commodity yet not always provided for in the curriculum. Above all he knew his patients, and their chief deadly complaints,—the rheumatism and the agueing fever. Then, of course, there were the accidents which occurred from time to time, chiefly in the harvest field. Some poor wight fell off a stack, or got caught up in the machinery of a thrasher, or got kicked by a horse, or a boy fell out of a tree when " buds nasin " ; and he would be called, post-haste, to set their limbs and ease their pain and soothe the agitation of their relations, which latter, in many cases, was of far greater moment than the fractures. But he was usually equal to the occasion, improvising splints out of the hedgerow for the unfortunates ; while an amputation in the open air was well within his ambit, as it received the open-mouthed approbation of the onlookers,—" I rackun he made a whooly good job o' owd Brabner's leg ; thet he did bor ! " Thus fulfilling a boyish ambition and that which had drawn him into the profession, for he had a strong affection for the saw and his kit of tools !

He had presided over the destinies of several parishes for more years than he cared to remember and sometimes felt as though he were a second father of all living. Then, of course, there was the accumulation at the various churchyards. He might have sent a few there before their time in his young days ; but in the main, he had but acted as a sort of umpire, whose decisions were arranged for him, but were none the less final ! All the same the tale was mounting.

No telephone in his day, thank God ! Folks' ills weren't all that urgent ; complaints were of the five miles an hour variety, and could bide a while ; leastwise until the morning ! For as the doctor said to the boy who had called him out of bed to see his mistress and was not satisfied with the doctor's pace,—

" Ah, yar, bor—If trotten ont save her, galloppen ont ! " None of your " blitzkriegs " then, thank you !

and even that old blusterer, influenza, was made to foot it. But if so be that some kindly neighbour or distracted member of the household should ride post haste and ring his rusty bell in the middle of the night, good Bailey was not above sticking his night-capped head out of the window, and, half asleep, enquire,—" What's troubling you, bor ? "

"All right, I'll come, wait while I saddle the mare." And they would clip-clop off together, five, six, seven miles away, in any old weather, and he back at day-break !

He lived in that picturesque little house just inside Yoxford, with its battlemented bay windows of little squared panes of glass that shine so clearly even on a wet day. It has just the suggestion of a fortress ; and such it was to him, for from here he fought the ills of the countryside with his electuaries and syrups.

His surgery was a snug little room, with its warm red curtains ; it would be considered far too snug to-day with our eye on dust traps and our senses attuned to hygienics. With, in winter, a nice fire crackling up the chimney and a strong smell of tobacco. A warm-looking table-cloth on the table, and a lamp casting a shadow about the outskirts of the room, adding a contribution to the scent of tobacco and drugs. But it did at least make you feel comfortable when you entered feeling that all was not well with you and that you might perchance be calling in here to see Bailey just before paying a lengthier visit to the churchyard. In fact, you were apt to be so wooed out of your fancies that any medicine he dosed you with was as water to the duck.

In the dark recesses were his bottles of coloured mixture, or rather the coloured fluids from which the mixtures were compounded. And they do say, but one cannot always give credence to hearsay, that the cupboard that stood in the other recess held a fully articulated, grinning skeleton ; which might or might not have been the earthly frame of old Larter the smuggler, who was killed at the Sluice on one of his runs. The tale seemed to get about after a visit made to the surgery by Dobbler Brown, who, finding himself alone, awaiting the doctor's return, took it upon himself to open the cupboard door, just to satisfy his curiosity. Dobbler was that scared he could hardly wait for Bailey's return, and when he eventually came into the room and Bailey felt his pulse he asked him why he'd been running !

On the mantel-shelf was a brass pestle and mortar, a couple of stick stethoscopes, a cupping dish, and a tin rack for long clay pipes.

In that funny little nest of assorted drawers, made out of sweet chestnut, propped up on a table on the other side of the room, no two drawers being quite the same size, he kept all kinds of medicines and powders,—belladonna, calomel, aconite, sassafras, jalap, tartar emetic, dandelion, ginger, garden angelica, and the like. Hemlock for the chincough ; Hellebore for the worms ; Digitalis for the dropsy ; and lots and lots of jalap ! And surely, somewhere behind the curtains, and in the dark corners, there lingered the shades of the old worthies of his craft and mysteries,—Hippocrates, Linnæus, Fuller, Cullen, Gerard, and that powerful pair, Sydenham and Lewis !

And so the stream of that peculiar humanity that is Suffolk, found its way into his rooms—a curious mixture of cunning, superstition and kindly faith. More often than not his ear-ringed, tanned patients were openly wearing the old cramp-rings made from coffin handles, and he well knew they were carrying the cramp bones, often human ones, in their pockets, yet they came to him to relieve them of their rheumatics. And he knew the women were not above using chants and bits of coloured threads to ward off this or that. And he dosed them one and all with a generous hand, for there was nothing of the homoeopath about him or they. Plenty of jalap and big blue pills ; big enough for an " owd hoss." For when Button asked him, " wud yew gi' me one o' yare owd scourers, for my owd innards fare thet tight " ; he wanted " suffen he cud swaller, thet he did ! " And Bailey saw he had it.

And he would listen to the tale of their complaints, which as he sometimes said might have been set to music, recounted as they were in that sing-song upper register.

" My hid dew fare kinder like a pomp ; thet goo up and down, yes thet dew ! "

" Can yew giv' me suffen fur Joe ? He ha' gort a naasty push on his arm, and thets all ablaze."

" My owd gal ha' gort a nasty tissickin cough, and hare stroop is that scratchy ; she fare sometimes as thew she'd quackle."

" He runned a thistle prick in his finger an' that dew agitate sew ; thet be makin' a' absy."

" He cut hisself roight deep, but ta wownd roved oova good tidd'ly."

But Bailey was not confined to his surgery, for he seemed to carry it about on horseback, the horse which he used before he had that smart little gig. From here he was not above looking at their old tongues and feeling their pulses, out in the open air, in the corners of the fields in which they worked.

It need hardly be said that his patients were all living persons, their individual selves and not merely numbers on a card, recorded and kept in a little receptacle called a " file " ; producing an income for the doctor whether well or sick. True they were not punctilious in their payments, but for that matter, neither was he at all diligent in sending out accounts, besides, most of them couldn't read if he did ! Money and income had not emasculated him into a state

I

servant nor reduced his charges to the level of a panel. He and they retained their souls with little or no thought of rewards and settlements. Neither did he go from one cottage home to another, with an eye for the best bits with which to adorn his own home. Not he, he was the doctor, not a disguised higgler masquerading as an apothecary.

Of course he had to be careful with his dosing, well knowing they preferred " smuggler's medicine," but what he did administer in large and liberal doses, was swallowed in faith, which was as great in efficacy as any of the drugs, although Coué was then unknown. Besides, there was always that little pertinent note in his herbal book, pencil-lined, and solidly true,— " these medicines have been given in some cases without success,"—which is more reasonable of acceptation than the oft-repeated dictum of the Trade journals— " The operation was entirely successful, but the patient died."

Bailey hadn't many friends ; companionship was limited, but there was a deep and mutual admiration between himself and the parson. The squire was just that degree beyond, although they were not above sharing a bottle together and talking over " hosses," or the prospects for the Twelfth. Besides, did he not use the balling gun on the squire's favourite mare with great effect, thereby earning for himself the squire's eternal gratitude ? And did he not keep that special dose for the squire, labelled " *Teucrium marum*," the powdered leaves of which according to the learned Murray is best given in wine ! But with the parson it was different, for both saw human nature in its elemental state, and understood it. After all, Bailey's gig usually appeared outside the little homes to herald arrivals or outgoings, and the parson had a good deal to do with that sort of thing. True, parson's books weren't much in Bailey's line, but for that matter, drugs and smells weren't much in the parson's way, but they shared an interest in the common folk, and had many a laugh together over the characters and customs. Bailey, too, was a good mimic, and his recapitulation of the day's visits and experiences was greatly appreciated by the parson, when, perhaps, the two were sharing one of Bailey's numerous geese.

" I've been to see poor old Betsy Rouse to-day who has a mighty bad leg. There she was, poor old soul, huddled up in her chair, as close to the fire as she could get, her old face as red as her legs, which were perched up on another chair.

" 'How d'ye fare now ? ' ses I, and out came her old sing-song drone, I thought at first as how she was going to sing,—

" 'I ha gort sitch a lamentable push on my lig, an' thet boolk [throb] sadly ; an' at night thet itch an' thet pritch fit tew craze on'. I fare as thew I cud tare it tew bits, thet I dew, or scurry [scour] it wi' an owd hoss comb. Thet's a rum un, thet is ! '

" 'Oh,' says I, ' I'll see if I can give you summat for that. A little bit to rub on it. Have you washed it lately ? I suppose when you were a you. girl you wouldn't have asked the doctor about it ? ' Her old face brightened up and she gave me a grin, as she said,—

" 'No thet I wudna', my owd mother wud a seen tew thet. She'd a gone and got a little suffen from the sheep's pens and mixed thet wi suffen out o' the holl and she'd a soon ha' cured thet. But thare, thare, times hev changed, thet they hev, and I fare tew warsh myself thet offen as I ha' whooly scared my poor owd mother. But if you'll send me suffen I'll be right glad ; and thank 'ee ; thank 'ee ; I'll take it right kind on 'ee! ' "

Like the parson, Bailey was very fond of his garden, his flowers, and his trees. Old fashioned, perhaps, the slightest bit wild, but as fragrant as a passing shower or burst of sunshine could make it. Mossroses, sweet-

William, phlox; fat fragrant roses, wallflowers, velvety
pansies, picotees, peonies, satin-stemmed pinks ; with
a background of evening primroses ; not forgetting a
rambling, roving, deliciously smelling bed of mignonette.
Then, of course, there was the lavender, balm and box,
with a tree of bay to mellow the whole and provide a
leaf or two for the milk puddings.

His pears were his especial pride, his Jargonelles, and
not least, the cookers, that old tree against the wall ;
old long before he became a doctor, cultivated and
brought to perfection by another doctor, as long ago
as the end of the seventeenth century—Uvedale St.-
Germain, which were so kind to his palate in the dull
and empty days of January, and lasted wellnigh to
Easter.   And the Black Fig, of which Mrs. Bailey was
so fond, that flourished exceedingly, perhaps because
it kept such close company with the midden heap near
its roots.

The apples that caught the sun and seemed to hold
it in their shining skins—Sops o' Wine ;   Jennetings ;
pippins, Blenheims, and the lovely russet.   These later
would be transferred to that little closet upstairs, tucked
away behind the rambling old chimney and which
would hold the fragrance, distilled by sun and rain, the
whole year round.

Then there were the strawberry beds, about which the
bees fussed and which later produced such huge, fat.
ruddy heart-shaped fruits that reminded him somewhat
of the stubbly, rubicund faces of his patients.   Neverthe-
less he swallowed them if it did feel just a bit canni-
balistic ;   although Bessy's cream helped to dispel the
illusion.

But, perhaps, his especial pride was the pretty little
chit of a tree, which grew at the end of the lawn.   A
twisted, slender bit of a stem, no thicker than the wrist
of a good-sized man, which slanted up for some four
feet before it twisted itself into a rounded bush of

foliage. This quince was a thing of sheer beauty ; in spring with its single blossoms, bedecking the new green so akin to the wild rose, lingering out blossom time by being last. And then later in the season with its mellow fruits hanging like Chinese lanterns in a bottle sky.

But Mrs. Bailey had an equal pride in the tree, and watched its progress through the years with a jealous eye, for she was a rare practitioner at jams and jellies, as her husband at medicines. The brand " Quince," written in crabbed and tiny letters on the little labels, had an honoured place both on pantry shelves and at table. Mrs. Bailey was wont to receive her guests with her own particular ritual; taking a cue from her husband's habits with his patients she " dosed " them on arrival. First, she'd give them a spoonful of quince jam, to be followed immediately by a glass of her cowslip wine, with the result they felt right " bobbish " and knew their welcome. Not last year's vintage ; oh, no ! Nor the year before that, for it was ten years gone since those flowers nodded amid the grass on the lawn. Six pounds of " blows " to ten gallons of water was her remedy, and the resulting colour would have gladdened the heart of the most earnest seeker after that elixir which so eluded the old chemists. Cowslip wine, stored on that cool brick floor of the capacious pantry, in those queer-shaped apoplectic-necked bottles, smugglers' remainders, that probably held " suffin " stronger than " paigle " when they were trundled, late at night, up the sedgy river.

Yes, Bailey was fond of his garden, whether early in the morning, when dew pearls were still weighing down the leaves or sliding into creamy throats. When an occasional and passing dragon-fly would plane through on a wide circuit from the marshes. Or, late in the evening, a bit " riled like " after listening to so many people's complaints, he would sit in the honeysuckle-covered summer-house, set in the corner of the gardən, and listen,—

> There pipes the wood-lark, and the song-thrush there
> Scatters his loose notes in the waste of air.

THE PARSON

> The Psamists man of yeares hee lived a score,
> Tended his flocke all one ; theire offspring did restore
> By Water into life of Grace ; at font and grave,
> He served God devout : and striv'd men's soules to save.
> He fedd the poore, lov'd all, and did by Pattern showe,
> As pastor to his Flocke, ye way that they shoulde go.

WE'VE had a deal of parsons in our village, since Ulf or Adam, William or Joes, but they have been known less for themselves as by the "midda," which is, and has been through all the long years, part of their patrimony. And, after all, Parson's Meadow is a lovely bit of our parish, as lovely a trifle of Suffolk as you could find. So much so, that if all the rest of England fell away in some astronomical cataclysm, and only the parson's meadow, with its bit of sky, was left swinging in space it would be identified by the Recording Angel as being of Suffolk.

It stands at the corner of the ways, where the old moss-grown sign-post points ; one, to the Street and Church ; two, to the Ford and the sea ; the other to Yew Tree corner and the turnpike. And it was there when the road was only a Pack-Way, or a Roman street, and one part went straight on up the Back Road Hill across the " Carnser," while the other fork went up past the Manor House, on through the Wash to the Pack-Way and Kelsale. The old Ford used to cause a deal of trouble in the winter for it would persist in spreading itself out and creeping up as far as the old sign-post and the gate to the meadow.

But someone, " God rest his soul in Heaven full merrily ! " planted those smooth-boled beech, and that copper beauty, under which the cattle linger in the heat of summer, and which screen the road almost to darkness. Then you must know, too, that our river runs through the meadow ; slowly and softly, past the boundary of the

Parson's garden, and that fine screen of trees which shut the Rectory in, holding in its smiling, muddy depths, between the lilies, forget-me-nots and sedges, eels and pike, roach and dace, Jack-o'-lanterns and Mermaids, as it babbles on to the wild-fowls and the sea. That could tell some rare tales if that could speak. How, wearing those great old boots that crinkled up to the shape of their thighs, they used to bring the old kegs along at dead of night—and drop one in for parson, or a bit of silk for his lady—to show there was no ill feeling. For it is still known as " Rackford Run."

No, they never stacked the tubs under the altar of our church, that happened a little lower down the Run, for our river served a goodish wide circuit with its cargoes, including that collection of red roofs which is East Bridge.

One end of the meadow is marshy, but that adds to its beauty when the mists rise at evening and wrap themselves about the tops of the one or two stumpy willows ; and the green is full of meadow-sweet and mare's-tails.

But Parson's meadow means more to the parish than all that, for here we have held the frolics from time out of mind. Coronations, jubilees, victories and " nubbady knows what." You could always know when a jollification was going on by the Band, perched up in one of those gaily coloured waggons, by the chink of the quoits, the wrestling, and the jumping of the river, and running races bare-foot. And " dew you mind when ole Sam a sloshed hisself in the water, when he got kind o' unsunsible drunk, and we had a good tidy job a gitten him out ? I tuk old o' his hid and Joe tuk his fit, and we gort him home thus'n."

Yes, we have had a " hape " o' parsons. There were those fellows sent here by the old Abbot ; " botty " chaps they were, for our church belonged to the old Abbey at Leiston yonder. But then there were two churches, both in the same churchyard, and they used

to get that jealous of one another as never was.   As soon
as one parson went in to commence the service, the other
would go and ring his bells, until there was such a to-do
that the old Bishop said there was only to be one church
so the other was pulled down.

Yes, ours is a lovely, sleepy churchyard.   It almost
seems as though the whole village had drunk deep of
distilled poppies ; those poppies, blood red, which grow
amid the   corn with such wonderful effect in that
upland field yonder ; and of a truth these folk who
lie here under the old leaning lichened stones and grave
boards, are but asleep.   Should the Trump sound, and
these hummocks and old graves burst asunder, the
motley contents would find themselves strangely at
home.   This one would be looking for his pightle,
another for the pulk from which she got her water.
This one for his mill ; but then, alas, he of the company
would be sad, for it has gone !   But the blacksmith
would find his fire still sparkling—and who knows ?—the
smuggler his load, just where he left it.   A drop of his
" suzzles " would be right good and hearty in these days
of shortage and " under-proof."   If he offers us a drop
we'll see we won't swobble it !

One thing we should notice about the throng would
be the large number of sailors—real sailors—"maryners,"
some with the signs of their drowning still about them.
None of your " turnpike-sailors," but those who knew
every wind of heaven, every sandbank along this
treacherous coast, and every church steeple.   To say
nothing of the Iceland traffic, the marauding pirates and
the " Waftage " of the Royal Navy.   These are they out
of the crayers, pinks, " fisshyng-botes " and " jackass "
schooners, for which these parts have been famous, and
who lived so close to nature and the heavens, but withal,
were not above a bit of piracy themselves.   They might
have had a boat with a pious name and a very innocent
look ; but as a man is known by his deeds, so were these

ships by the rascals who manned them, and the exhibitions of their sometime bad temper.

And there would be the " Priests and Deacons " gathering their robes about them, complete with taper and bell, making a bee-line for the church lest they be late for the morning Mass. Except that one, surely a doctor, who is having a few words with old Bedwell for having appropriated his memorial stone for his own obsequies. But then, as Bedwell says, cap in hand—

" Well, master, yow didn't raise no objection when I found it, a diggin' owd Goody Rous's grave. I thowt thet wor tew good a stone tew throw away or be put down to be tramped ower by folk's grut owd butes, so I had thet cut up ready, kinder. Besides I thowt thet ud look just right in our owd Church yard ; that seemed tew fare match the owd Church. Thare yew ken hev thet back right quick. I doan't fare tew warnt thet no more ! "

" Oh, no thank you, Bedwell. But I did feel annoyed when I heard you tampering about with it. You see, he was one of the best masons round here for miles who designed and cut out that Cross. I see it has stood well all these years."

" Yes, thet thet hev, Master. I allus did admire thet. But there I must gew and see what hev become o' my owd hoss. The seal o' the day tew yew, Master ! "

" Good-morning, Bedwell ! "

It would have been, surely, a thousand pities if we had lost these characters for ever, which might have been the case if we had no church yards and ours in particular. It seems to be the argument against cremation, for what can one evoke from a mere handful of dust ? Not impossible, true, but very difficult ! You see, the bones of old Sanders of Dunwich, " Master," under God, of the barque " Jamys," might come together with a rattle and articulate into none other than he. For don't you recall, he had a slight stoop and how one arm was longer than

the other ? But that may have been because of the
" 44 butz of bier at 13/4 the butz," which he took with
him on his " viage " to Iceland in 1545.

Let us hope we may find him here amongst the motley,
for he will be able to tell some rare tales of to and from
to Iceland after ling and cod, in those cockles that passed
for ships. But of course the chances are he may not be
here ; his old carcass may be a few miles " fudder " off,
on one of those sandbanks or maybe, the Shipwash !

" But it's a long toime since we hed such a good passon
as the one we've gort now. He ha bin hare a mort o'
yares, his hare be a gittin' roight mouldy a top. He's
whooly different tew the one afore him. Orl he thowt
on wor a racin' thro' the sarvice as hard as he coud
gew wi' his grut owd butes on, and then a tarin' orf his
sarplice an' taring orf arter them owd hounds. Reglar
rum un, he wur. No, nawthin' like thet about Master,
but he dew prach sich long sarmons ; shakes us ower the
Pit regular ewey Sunday and sees as how nobody goes
tew sleep. If he dew catch anyone a noddin he blare
owt fit tew wake the dead, and puts ewery one in a
regular dudder. I sot unner a wimmun once who wor
a pracher, but I cuddent nohows git on wi hare. Tew
much loike listenin tew my owd wummun ; an she's
enough fur me ! No, gie me owd passon an is ell !
Perhaps yew've heerd thet tale about the wummun as
couldna sleep at night, so she used tew gew an hare
summun prach as wud send hare tew slape. Well, thet
didna happen hare in this parish.

"I ken jest recall when he cum hare. I wur a little
bit o' a boy then, but I ken remember the grut owd
waggins, six on em, as browt his things from Walpole
way. Word fared tew git round as how the new parson
hed cum, so we all trooped off and garped, thet we did ! "

Hamilton was perhaps the best parson we had for
many years. He came in that transition period of the
Church, following hard after the heels of the indifferent,

roistering parsons ; the evangelical serious men with
large beards and un-Oxford collars, who took their jobs
seriously, and, too often, seriously too, the restoration
of their mouldering churches, preferring pitch-pine to
old oak and brightly coloured glass to the faded ambers of
the former years.

Needless to say, Hamilton knew everyone in the
village and it was fatal to let him see you setting off to
pritch for eels on a Sunday ; he would want to know
what you were after. For as he would say, the country
might be lovely, but that is just where the devil likes to
be ; for the " owd davil " is " whooly fond o' trees, and
apples and young wimmin." " But thare the davil
didna seem tew come near him ; fared tew be tew
scared. Dew yew carl tew mind when we didna hev
no rain fur weeks ? Passon calls a special sarvice an
offers up prayers ; my hart thet he did ; an the owd rain
cum sumpin down the werry next day. I rackun thet
put an ind tew the devils kernivers, thet thet did."

But Hamilton was at his best probably, when there was
trouble in the house and someone was " upstairs." He
would come in very quietly with all kinds of kind
enquiries, and what had Bailey said ? for he was very
fond of Bailey. And if so be the two should meet at a
patient's bedside they would fall to talking as if there
was no stopping them. It was so when they met at
Josh Baggot's who had the jaundice which had turned
him as yellow as a " paigle," and they fell to talking of
" Christy Anthems." Hamilton said as how he'd got
some as yellow as Josh. Bailey wouldnt have that,
because he said if that was so then he'd have to come
and give them some of his calomel ! And then they
laughed together, and Josh, too, until he nearly turned
another colour.

And then there was the time when old Noller nearly
went off his head ; and sad to say, his old woman was
helping him the way he was going all she could. She

kept running to the bottom of the stairs and bawling up until he was raving. Someone called in the parson and he came as quick as he knew how, for they were expecting the cart from the House. First of all he set about Noller's missus and sent her a going—" the duzzy fule "; then he went upstairs, while everyone was a " garpin " with fear as to what Noller would do. Hamilton made a mental note of the room, noticed the bed was against the wall, so he persuaded Noller to get into bed again and promptly sat on the outside of the bed nearest the stairs and Noller couldn't get out. Then he began to talk to Noller about his garden and his roses, as though there was nothing amiss. Then he began to sing, and his top notes made Noller laugh, though presently Noller began to sing too, and before Hamilton left Noller was as right as could be, having received a solemn promise from the parson that he would see to it that he would never go to the dreaded House.

But Hamilton was always a bit funny where women were concerned ; he could nohows abide those who were " as smart as a carrot, but as empty as a skep " ! And he was rather down on the " mawthers " who were wedded (grass widders, we called them) before their " sybbits " were called. But they always brought their little ones to him to be christened ; and sometimes they had the mind to ask him to see their chaps and make them marry them ; and he always did. But he used to like going to see the old cronies—old Aunt Rebecca, for instance—and watch her fine stitches and drink a cup of her tea. It didn't make any difference to him that she went to chapel ; in fact he said the chapel sharpened his wits and kept the village from growing dull and stale. Some of his best friends went to that ugly old chapel, and his gardener was one. Besides, as he said, it wasn't the label you had on that mattered, but whether " yare owd bundle hed fallen off into the holl," like Bunyan's Christian whom he was for ever quoting.

Sometimes when he could nohow make a sermon he would go off and see the Prophet, and ask him what he thought of so-and-so. What would he say, for instance, if he were going to preach from " It is good for me that I have been in trouble " ?

" Well," says John, " I doant fare tew think as how yew ken know much about that. I rackun I cud prach a better sarmon from thet then yew ken. Yew see, Master, I've bin in it, and I doant fancy yew hev."

" But ah ! John, there you make a mistake. Do you remember the text which says—' the heart knoweth its own bitterness ' ? " And so they would fall to hammering it out between them, and the village would know the result the following Sunday !

On one occasion when Hamilton was away, old Doctor White came to preach for him. A very learned man was the doctor and he preached a very learned sermon. When he returned, Hamilton made it his business to ask Pepper the clerk what he thought of the sermon ? " Wunnerful," says Pepper ; " the most wunnerful sermon I ever heered ; but I can't say as how I roightly unnerstood a wud ort." That made Hamilton laugh ; he said he wished his old friend Barham had heard it ; he'd have made something of it, he expected.

Needless to say Parson lives in the Rectory, a pleasant Georgian house of two stories, of which the garden was laid out by his immediate predecessor, including the magnolia-grandiflora, immediately in front of the entrance door, which is such a lovely harbinger of spring with its fine waxy petals. It is a comfortable little home which welcomes you straight into a little room with a classic fireplace set in between two domed-shaped cupboards filled with Mrs. Hamilton's china, set out on the nicely-shaped shelves. On the right-hand side is the dining room cum library, for here along the walls are Parson's books, of which he has good store, not forgetting that one volume next in importance to Bible

and Prayer-book, " The Complete Tything Table "
(Proper for all Vestries, Clergymen and Gentlemen's
Halls). Here are a pair of cheffoniers that are part of
the house and simply shine in their own splendour.
Behind this is the drawing-room, where hang one or
two family portraits, little cameos of ensigns in red
jackets, and at least one Bishop, complete with frilly
lawn sleeves and a seraphic countenance. This room
opens into the garden through the glass lean-to that
runs along the whole side of the house.

The kitchen quarters are completely cut off by a red
baize-covered door, on the other side of which, along a
wide stone-flagged path, is the pantry, which you reach
by mounting two or three smooth white stairs, for it is
built over the cellars. A large pantry in keeping with
the large kitchen and the immense kitchen table that
seem to speak of accommodation and disposal of tithe
in kind, and a large and liberal diet.

Near the pantry was the schoolroom, where the
young Hamiltons received instruction before passing to
training Academies for the Army and Navy. Amongst
these was that young scamp of a George Washington
Hamilton. He noticed that his mother came down
regularly with the ritual of his father, to unlock the
pantry door. Watching his opportunity, and with a
stealth, later to be of service to him in the field, he
managed to " bop " in without being seen and to gulp
down a mouthful or two of jam. Hastily retreating,
wiping his mouth, plebeian like, with that part of the
hand not so used, he endeavoured to dispose of what
he took to be the string of the pot cover, but which he
found, to his disgust, was the tail of a mouse that had
forestalled him. Which, of course, saved him from a
thrashing and cured him of petty larceny for the rest
of his life.

Upstairs are the bedrooms, daintily white with
dimity and chintz, comfortable with best goose feathers

and linen sheets, and lit by square-paned windows that
let in the sun and against which the China roses thrust
their fragrant bosoms.

Hamilton was very proud of his garden which he, or
rather Noah, kept to the best of his ability. Hedges all
nicely cut, trees trimmed, paths clean as Dunwich
beach, and the lawn as fine and smooth as his black
coat. Noah used to cut this with his scythe which he
could swing as steady and as cleanly as his razor.
Flower beds, rose-covered archways, kitchen garden
and wilderness, made up a pleasuance set amid a screen
of great trees, bounded towards the river by the coach
house and stables of faded red brick with lunettes that
gave it an almost ecclesiastical appearance, as befitted
the domain of a parson of the Established Church.

Mrs. Parson was inclined to be somewhat stately,
that is as stately as anyone can be who possesses a full
face tending towards the rubicund. She had strong
views on sex—a thing almost unknown in our village—
and when some boys had the temerity to select that
portion of Rackford Run which abuts on the vicarage
gardens, and there bathe *in puris naturalibus*, there was
such an outcry as never was. It was her part in the
domestic economy to write any family letters that
required to be written. To arrange audiences with
any poor relations—one in particular, a lame scion
who walked with one only crutch, and who according
to the laws of society, had married beneath him—
though it was the best job he ever did in life—and
refused to be shipped off to Canada or Australia in
expiation. He was summoned into the presence twice
annually to receive a welcome £5 note on each occasion.
If all was well he would be addressed as " Dear Edward "
but if not, then as " Dear Mr. Hamilton." From which
you will gather that Bailey was not the only one who
kept skeletons.

Yet, she was no mean helpmeet to the Rector, could

provide the most succulent soups and was not above
sitting up all night with some lonely sad soul whose day
was done, but whose passage lingered. And was she
not on visiting terms at the Hall and entitled to receive
the " bops " or curtseys of the village maidens ? Which
was a source of some satisfaction to be included amongst
the amenities of life. And she would give a dose or
two out of her own medicine chest : salts and senna tea,
ipecacuanha and the hated, loathed castor-oil. Would
preside over an administration of brown-paper plaster,
covered with tallow for the hairy chest ; and, not least,
dill water for the babes. Her activities in these directions were rather frowned on by Bailey who considered
she was poaching on his preserves, but there, he had
little to worry in this unpaid function of apothecary's
assistant ; and as he said she was welcome to a double
portion of his indigestion at Michaelmas.

And there was one day in high summer, when all the
village was *en fête*, and which for convenience might be
called Hamilton's day or Hamilton's Feast. This was
the occasion when all who possibly could, men, women,
children, were taken by him to spend the day by the
sea at Dunwich. The farmers would lend their waggons
and horses which would be decorated with any finery
that was forthcoming. He would take no excuses, and
almost haled out of bed the bedridden ones for the
occasion ; he even constrained poor old Nan Rouse to
make the trip when she was ninety-four. It was a very
merry procession along the dusty, gritty roads, behind
the broad backs of the horses, sweating and flicking
their long tails, their bits of brass shining in the sun,
and colours flying from the carters' whips. Tea was
served in the Noah's Ark, an old timber erection on
legs, standing all too near the cliff's edge ; and a photograph—yes, a photograph—taken of the whole group
with the old nettice that stood by the crumbling churchyard of the ruined church as background. My word,

K

what a parlarvering it was to get that picture " took " —arranging and re-arranging ; trying to get Broom and Button and Aunt Rebecca and Cousin John into focus, all grouped round Hamilton who was plump in the middle of what he liked to describe as " his children." And what an old-fashioned lot they look to-day, with bonnets and shawls, and wide-awake hats, and whiskers. Some serious as befitted such an ordeal, others smiling from ear to ear, and one actually waving a stick in the exuberance of the occasion. And then the return journey with the sun westering behind the elms beyond Yoxford, with the plain of Suffolk rolling peacefully inwards and onwards towards the heart of England.

No, Hamilton didn't die in our parish after all, but they brought back his old " carcass " to be buried here amongst his friends in the place he knew and loved so well. He went away just as they sold the advowson, the man who bought it being persuaded that as Hamilton was turned eighty, might be reasonably considered to be on his last legs. But Hamilton knew better and lived to see ninety-five and dished the lot because he had an interest in the living to his dying days.

IN " SARVICE "

Why, that there daater 'a yars grow a fine swaken gal.
Ah, she dew—she'll be a wappa if she git on thussen's.
Wha's she the pitman, eh ?
Iss—no—why I don't fare ta know—she's a twin—I've the
fulla tew 'ar a toom.

MAJOR ED. MOORE.

THE village maiden has been credited with more vices
than virtues. If we accept Crabbe, and others for that
matter, her blooming cheeks, ruby lips, laughing eyes
and swelling bosoms, acted but as a screen for a freedom
in morals. This, it is good to say, has not been borne
out by the facts. To be poor, to be brought up as one
of a large family, in one of those tiny cots which formed
the countryside of Suffolk, and to be conversant with
elemental nature from early childhood, was not to be
depraved or coarse, for as Washington Irving observed
in his day (1819) there was " a degree of taste and
elegance in rural economy that descends to the lowest
classes." There are exceptions to every rule, but one is
proud to think that so much fineness came out of such
unpromising circumstances. Of course there were other
eyes than Crabbe's ; there was, for instance, his con-
temporary Bloomfield ; and such artists as Woodford,
Biggs, Morland and Smith. And it is the latter's
Wood Nymph that one prefers to associate with the
English country scene, rather than the *Phoebe Dawson*
of the too often crabbed Crabbe.

The large family, the straitened circumstances,
tended to that dispersal of the brood, such as is seen
every spring in our hedgerows. At an early age, out
into the world to seek that fortune, good or ill, which
awaits the traveller. And in the days of early and
mid-Victoria, it was to " Sarvice " that the Suffolk

girl must go ; which might lead by easy stages, or by one fell jump, to the city of Babylon itself.

Eliza was no exception ; the eldest of the clutch, she must be the pioneer, and venture forth into the unknown. Young, very young, but of a strong character, built on the stocks of old Suffolk, containing in her young veins the blood of Vikings, Danes, Saxons and Normans, in mixed but unpolluted strain. Some elements of " larning " had she gleaned at the Dame's school, supplemented by the Sunday school, and that wisdom which is held in local customs, and the lore that passes from mouth to mouth. A certain amount of freedom had been hers, though not much, for there were younger ones to look after, and as her mother once wrote— " You was all brought up to work some sort, and it never hurt you." But her great consolation was her old donkey, on whom she went for many a gallop on errands or to help her father in the work of the farm. She had two donkeys in her time, Reuben and Jack, and with these she would peddle coal, obtained in bulk at Darsham station, in a little cart, picked up with the donkey, at some sale or the other. Even this sort of enterprise was not without adventure, as on the occasion when she, with her sister, perched up on the bags of coal, were coming down the hill from Middleton Moor, and Reuben began to kick. He showed those two gals what he thought of them, and seemed as though he had taken leave of his senses as he would of the cart. However, scrambling off in quick time, they managed to get him quiet, when he proceeded on his way as though nothing had happened.

Then there were visits to Grandmother, for she was " ullus " Grandmother's gal, and almost lived down there at Ratley Corner, for she liked a peep at her bird, in its wicker cage, mayhap a canary or a King Harry. Then, too, Grandmother kept bees, and made mead out of the honey-comb, and maybe, she'd give you a little

drop, or, maybe, a sip of herb tea. Grandmother, of
course, was as poor as poor could be, but she liked a
drop of tea, and when she went to the Hall to do the
washing up (six in the morning to six at night, for
sixpence a day) she'd see if they'd got any fine china
cups with the handles off, for tea " ullus " tasted better
out o' they. Then she'd pour out just half a cup, no
milk or sugar, put a spoonful of sugar in her mouth and
let the raw tea just trickle through the sweetness. But,
of course, Grandmother was always at work, scraping
up a few coppers, so she wouldn't have to miss giving
her Class money at the chapel. Maybe she was mending
sacks, coarse old hempen sacks, with a large needle that
made a kind of circular darn. Where's my mantle
(apron) she would say, as she set to work, first donning
this little bit of a thing that tied round the waist, and
then again half way up the skirt, that old rusty black-
green skirt that hardly seemed to need a mantle to
preserve it. Then she used to mangle clothes for a few
coppers, or attend to those as were " near their time·"
And there was always " Old Fly," the dog.

Life was punctuated by a few frolics ; there was the
Whit-tide tea at the chapel ; and the wonderful stall
which old Broom used to build outside his shop on the
Whit-Monday, to help religion at the chapel into a
joyous mood and his returns to a happier amount !
And that one day in seven, spent at the old square-faced
chapel, of sinister look but happy memory ! Not forgetting the festival of St. Valentine, when children got
up very early in the hope of catching someone. The
method was to greet some kind-hearted one with
" Good Morrow, Valentine," twice before they could
speak to you and if successful they must give a present.
But one always ran the risk of the reply—" You're
Sunburnt," especially if it was after the sun had risen.

There was a good deal of other worldness about
Eliza ; a good deal of reserve and aloofness which was

neither understood nor appreciated by her friends or relations ; but they could not enter into her thoughts or the quiet joys of self-communing. She would nestle down into her soft bed at night, in the room with all the brothers and sisters, a bit crowded, perhaps, and yet strangely and delightfully alone when the clothes were tucked about her, only her ears and mouth outside the sheets. Then, if she did not fall immediately asleep, she could listen to the little echoing sounds that travel on the scented still air across the fields. The aspens' melancholy chatter over the horse pond ; a dog barking in the distance, a pony clopping along the turnpike, the call of a reveller, the owls in the churchyard elms, or the whinny of a horse in the marshes. Then she could watch the moon dipping behind the mysterious, shapely trees in the distance, and then dream her dreams of all the to-morrows.

Then there were her friends, girls much like herself, with whom she would go a-gleaning or harvesting. Compare notes as to what new thing they would wear at " Wissun "-tide, and so avoid the unwarrantable liberties of passing birds. And, not least, the merits and demerits of possible husbands ; and that always productive field of conversation—other girls, their shortcomings and peculiarities.

There were too, her accomplishments of sewing and mending, and cooking, even the proper handling of clothes that have to be wrung out. These had to be pleated up fan-wise before being wrung. And there was always the injunction,—" Get the eyes out o' them thare taters, Liza ! " Ability to use her fingers deftly, either in the dressing of a doll, the plaiting of rushes into a basket, or the fashioning of wayside poppies into dolls or soldiers—according to taste. The repertoire of a thousand little sayings and customs gleaned from father and mother and repeated and cherished amid laughter and fun. How it was lucky if you put on a garment inside out (without knowing it, of course). And if you wore your petticoat lower than your frock it was a sign that father thought more of you than mother did. And how, if you broke two things in succession, you would always break a third. And nonsense rhymes like,—

> Ode Mrs. Mason she brok' a bason ;
> Ode Mrs. Frost ast how much did that cost ?
> Ode Mrs. Hillin she said 'twas a shillin' ;
> Ode Mrs. Brown said ;. No, half-a-crown ;
> Ode Mrs. Denny said twarn't worth a penny ;
> Ode Mrs. Nye said 'twas all a downright lie.

Or,—

> Gowden-bug, Gowden-bug, fly away home,
> Yar house is bahnt deeyown an' yar children all gone.

Or,—

> Hiccup sniccup—look up-right up—
> Three drops in a cup—is good for the hiccups.

And, with bated breath,—

> Nine hahnets (hornets) 'al sting·a hoss ta dead.

Or with a very definite belief,—

> If adders could hear, and Sloe-worms could see,
> Neither man nor beast would ever go free !

But 'Liza must needs earn her " keep," and that right early ; so, by recommendation from the parson, and not to be far from home, she was taken as a maid at the house of a Q.C. in the next village, some three miles away.

Housework in those days was a serious business. Take a large house with many rooms, and realise the only water supply to be a pump, either out in the yard, or in the scullery, and all the rooms to be supplied with water that must of necessity be carried by hand. Lamps to be cleaned and tended ; if carelessly done then fish-:ails would appear on the chimney glass ; a thousand ҝitchen utensils to be shone until one could see one's face in them ; and floors, with no coverings but a few rugs, that must be constantly scrubbed to maintain their whiteness. Added to this, cooking, waiting at table, dusting, mending, and one realises that domestic economy was as exact a science as the running of a large business to-day. No aids to cleanliness in those days, and it seemed as though more and more tasks were created ; of a truth, labour saving had not yet been born. Innumerable scuttles of coal and firing ; huge piles of plates and dishes to be carried backwards and forwards, and endless washings-up.

Early-rising, very ; in summer of no account, but in winter a considerable ordeal. Fires to light that seemed determined not to draw, and the master and missus likely to come down at any moment ; what would they say if they should find her not finished ! And then sundry washings in cold water with her chilblained hands that reduced them to the consistency of her cold feet.

But the Q.C. and his wife were the proud and happy possessors of another house, politely termed the town house but which in reality was set in one of the prettiest of London's suburbs. Actually in the Town area, but situate on the fringe of more country. To this other home they were accustomed to migrate at various seasons of the year, sometimes autumn, sometimes spring. Eliza, therefore, in due time found herself on her way to this most eventful of all places to join the family already there. A lonely girl ; a large box, some packages tied up in coloured handkerchiefs ; a noisy smoking engine, a very third-class compartment. But she could make the journey in a day ; from the quiet and peace of mediaeval Suffolk, from home and friends, to the glare and wickedness of London ! What a surge of feelings, but what a sure purpose overcomes the disquiet, with a confidence which we, to-day, speak of as coming from higher education. The journey is accomplished, and another brings her to the new house, where she finds a living in the basement and a resting place under the roof. Two extremes, characteristic of life.

This was life indeed, but it required a good deal of adjustment on the part of one's self before it could be lived or even appreciated. Tinged with the romantic, but how foreign ! People looked almost scared when you went into a shop and asked for a " dwile," or if they heard you calling a pancake a " froises " or the weather " raughty." Or harder still, looked at you as though, well, since you were so newly up from the country, then you must be a bit simple. But when the butcher's boy tried to take an unwarrantable liberty he got more than he bargained for, and from henceforward treated this one with marked respect. However, when one got a bit homesick at the end of the day, there was that wonderful triumph of mind over circumstance, accomplished by opening the " grut owd box " beside her bed, thus releasing a whiff of the Suffolk air which it still held, and from which would rise a little picture of home, perchance at tea time or just after a " bake." This before going to sleep. It was a sinister-looking box, covered with black shiny cloth and studded with coffin nails, made by Mr. Selfe the wheelwright to hold all one's worldly belongings, and was therefore a piece of home—a bit of Suffolk !

But there was no looking back. Primroses and cowslips might arrive in a little box in the spring to remind her of the woods and hedgerows ; of Selfe's farm, the Dove House or the Hawthorns. And that constant stream of cross currents, in the shape of closely worded epistles, written and over written, on all kinds of scraps of paper, written on the spur of the moment at odd times, until one was all but blinded in the reading. But they could not lure one back. It was good to hear the chatter of the old life,—

I know if you are going in for cleaning you will want some good butter. I wish I could bring it you so no expence, as I used at Yoxford.

Well, I have to tell you the schoolmaster has gone and left in debt a lot ; what rascals there are in the world. I hear he owe over £15. . . . Past three o'clock. I have just set in oven 2 loaves, with sago pudding, rhubarb pie, little piece of pork, little plain cake, few shorts. That's the lot this week. Will you come and taste how good ?

Your uncle Chambers is taken away rather sudden, he would have been 86 in February. Bess went in to help him upstairs as he felt rather queer, but they couldn't get him up so he died downstairs. Bailey said it was syncope, you will know what I mean if its not spelt right. He was buried last Saturday, father followed. Jonah, Bob., J. Marjoram, Button, Baker and Freeman carried him. Of course he was heavy, not laying in bed to waste at all ; he was took down the street in a cart.

Thank you, dear for your dear letter, how it did remind me of days gone by never to be no more here. Yes, dear, Susie is getting up the hill and you all, I am going down the other way. Well dear, I was glad to hear you all as well as you are. I can feel for you about your eyes and neck. Oh, yes, my eyes are no worse but have them aches in them in the night, but it seems like cold. I tie them up sometimes, as they get warm they are a little easier, but it is the way we have to go. I have had it so long dear child, that I dont have any faith in anything to cure them ; it is better than being blind. Don't you think it hurt your eyes by doing so much needle work ? Oh, my, I think you have done well to do what you have. Yes, I expect your dress look nice, very good indeed. I shall soon begin the warm nightdresses. I feel these frosts so, but I am so glad I can get up and wait on father these cold mornings. We have had a nice lot of the pieces of the old shed to burn. Got a ton of coals in, so have got the shed done rather small but a nice little one.

*   *   *   *

I dont know what to say about C. They have got a big looking glass and another piano, so have got two musics, and like to look smart, her hair all down and that bracelet that was four or five shillings. I told her I like to see her hair done up it look more becoming her age. I think I offended her about doing her hair. I told her she could not do or spend the time if she was at service.

And what do you think? Aunt Ling came over one day time C. was here, she is just the same. She is at that house, so haven't no rent to pay, so dont take any harm, but I must say I liked Aunt Mahala the best. Aunt is so blunt. Yes, we always got along very well, poor old dear.

* * * *

I shall soon have to be at home, but I shall go to chapel when I can, if only once in a while, if I am spared. I went twice on Sunday, heard Mr. Walker, but he is so low, dont go enough so I cant hear all only some, but it is better than being at home all the day. Lilie Clouting have a son and Mrs. John Newson at the Mill a son—two princes.

I went home with Aunt from chapel Sunday Afternoon, so I told her I had one from you, and she said I was to give her love to all and she will write some day, as you cant say a word hardly by the chapel, but I did not stay long. So dont you think I have done well on Sunday? I must give up and go up Timber Hill and have a game of shut-eye, so I will bid you goodnight. Tie your eyes up, perhaps they like warmth, mine do. I have ached so between my shoulders for days, afternoons especially, and round my neck. Rheumatism I expect. (Tuesday night.)

Drawing for ten Wednesday morning—had a good nights rest, had you? Had one of the warm night-dresses on ; rather cold to take off to dress. Beautiful morning at present. Tell Lie to put the sack on the bed to keep them warm, I will write her next if I can. to-night is Missionary meeting, but I cant go, it will be so cold to come home. I am best at home night now weather is so cold.

* * * *

As Monday is your birthday, will you kindly except of this small mite as I thought the peas from home would be a treat. It is a poor possett but it comes free as if it was greater with both our wishes for your birthday.

Oh, this hot weather, isn't it wonderful, but thank God, I feel better to work towards evening, but it make the beer go

out fast, I shall have to brew again before Susie come if it is
in the next month. I can't stop to say much as I want to
do this up. Hope you will all enjoy them. You'd better
wash the white-currants and gooseberries; I have, all my
white ones for wine before I can use them. Don't suppose
I shal hear Mark Guy Pearse, I cant go if it is so hot, enough
to make one ill. Hope you are getting on with your work;
I can't do much sewing, father's shirts all burst across the
back—the sweat. I can't put you an egg in, do I would, but
I feel as if I must, tell me if it break.

* * * *

I have sent you just a taste for a pie. Father have sent you
all his dear children a sweet, you must divide them as well as
you can. The ring, he said, was for Susie. My passage is
not done yet, Aunt is busy this week. Come and help me,
there's a dear; well you have enough to do yourself, I expect.
Well, perhaps it will be done next if Aunt can come, but the
paper is too good to put on this old place. They wont do
anything, every where is going to ruin, shocking!

* * * *

I was talking to father about what I said about the cape,
and he said he sure he should not have said about it costing
what it did till I see you about it; you would all think we
grutched the money. I wished I hadn't said what I did in
Susie's letter as she went with sister Lie to get it and paid.
But I dont know, sometimes I feel so low spirited and dont
care about much as I used to do; yet I can't always wear
what I have, year out, year in, and I like to have things a
little fit to be seen to go out with; but I hope you will look
over all I said, and think no more about it. Explain to Susie
and Lie what I said, somehow. I thought it a lot for me for
my old body to wear, perhaps I might have done more good
in it, giving it to some of you or some-one else that want it
more, but I have got it and I hope God will bless me with
health to wear it.

* * * *

Just a line as it does seem a long time since I had one from
you, not since you sent me the hamper. I am sure I enjoyed
what you sent and the wine came so very nice as it was just

what I then wanted. Father brought me one home from Lowestoft, how things do work.

Something seemed to tell me to write you as I am afraid some of you are not well and that you are wanting. Low cupboard, not much work, is it? So do pray tell us. I was saying, should liked to have sent the hamper up if we had a chance to send it to Darsham by some one that we could trust to see to it, as we have a few bullises on the trees, a few apples and a few potatoes, as they weigh so heavy by post; but dont seem to know how to manage it. I do hope you are well and all of you, and if you are writing to-day why you need not answer this. This is such an unsettled time of year to us here that it seem to unsettle us or me now being alone again. Can't help it, oh, what a changing world it is, yet how we cling to life and to be here as long as we can, don't we?

Now you understand, I dont say the hamper is coming, no, only I should liked to have sent it. Do you think you would get it without my letting you know when I have sent it off whenever we do send one? But dont you count of it, for it is only my thoughts, but I want to hear how you go on and if you need any assistance from us do not be afraid to say as Father will soon be putting it away, then he say he shan't have it to lend. We lent Broom 3£. about Whit-tide, he is glad to have us take it out in goods, and we may as well let our own have it if you need it. So there, that's my thoughts about it, dont want for the sake of asking.

* * * *

But one could look back from this great distance ot London and see it all as a little picture hanging on the wall of life. Here, indeed, was expansion, fulness, if one could only grasp the opportunity and stretch one's mind to the occasion; while there, life was small and limited—at least so she thought. Soon too, there were friends and excursions; wonderful sermons at the great chapel—now a church; fireworks at the Crystal Palace; brass bands, and the glamour of a thousand shops. Oh, no, there could be no return, especially as now there appeared the shape of things to come in the person of a young man. No, not a " joskin," or even a " Lunnener," for that matter, but an honest to goodness " shummaker," also from the country, dressed in his " broad best " for she only saw him on Sundays and that every other one. But he must be approved by mother and father first, so at that great annual home-going in high summer, for those all two brief weeks, he must be taken to meet the keen eyes of a countryman who could read character as he could read the skies. And then a " sarnter " through the fields and " middas " and a presentation to old friends and relations and then back to London, with perhaps one of those old linen sacks filled with the best that life can offer and sewed up as though it was never to be opened.

And so life began once more anew, in one of those little houses so much alike, and of which London was so full, and found such a difficulty in getting them all in. A home, half Suffolk, half somewhere else, but the greater half was Suffolk.

* * * *

Time passes ; sixty-odd years roll over that little house, with their attendant dust and fading. It is a basement house, one in a terrace very close to a railway station ; and the trains, steam trains, have been a friendly accompaniment to the years and the house. Time could be reckoned by them, as the engines stopped just outside the bedroom windows, whistles blew and doors slammed, either for top-hatted, black-coated workers in the morning, or for finely fashioned ladies during the day. While the wind blew running phrases through the aeolian harp of the telegraph wires. Yes, it was a pleasant enough neighbour during the hey-day of the railways. But now, somewhen in the dark days of 1940, it is not so good a companion, it is too close.

Downstairs in the basement sits an old lady, in a dingy room, still lit by an oil lamp, as when she first went there as a young woman. The windows are heavily draped, there is a little fire in the grate, and the old lady almost crouches into the hearth, sitting there in her basket chair with her Bible and spectacles. The sirens have sounded on this Sabbath evening, but she is fortunately deaf ; although as she says, she can hear when a bomb falls ! The guns are roaring for there is an evil angel abroad. Presently there is a whine, but she does not hear, then a roar and the place is full of dust and smoke, for a bomb has fallen directly on the house next door. It mercifully explodes instantaneously and does not penetrate, but the roofs of four houses are blown away and the upper stories wrecked. What of the old lady ? Is she upset ? Not unduly. She stands up in the fog which has suddenly sprung up in her rather dowdy room, waits for it to subside, then a voice rings clear—" Put that light out ! " the light being her old oil lamp, for the heavily hung windows are agape. Then she sits her down in her creaking chair and goes to sleep until the morning. And it was with the utmost difficulty that she could be persuaded to leave the old place. Certainly she would not have gone, but she was " foorst " ! The old Suffolk stubbornness was still strong in the blood.

And so, per bomb, she returned to live in that air and under those skies which gave her birth ; to those fields that had echoed to her play and her girlish songs. And in returning to her nativity so she grew young again inspired by the memories of the years !

VOCABULARY

Ablaze—inflamed.

Buds-Nazin—bird's-nesting.
Blows—blossoms.
Bachus—backhouse or scullery.
Bavin-fork—fork for bavins, light loose faggots.
Butes—boots.

Chill—to take off the chill.
Closing-in-time—twilight.
Chaney—chintz or china.
Cuppey-whayed—go to the left.
Cromed—dragged in.   Crome—hook.
Cruden-barrow—wheelbarrow.
Christy-anthem—c h r y s a n t h e-mum.
Creepled—settled.

Dows—pigeons.
Dwiles—dishcloth or floorcloth.
Dibbled—seed sown with dibbling iron used by man walking backwards, children following and dropping 3 or 4 grains of seed into hole made by the iron, by means of thumb and finger.
Drift—a lane, often sunken, that leads nowhere in particular.

Fansets—see also Spickets.
Fletchets—young peas.
Fleeters—skimmers.
Fourses—snack at four o'clock in the harvest-field.

Gotch—large jug or vessel.
Gimmer—hinge.
Garpin—staring.

Hens-nose-full—little bit, very small amount.
Holl—dry ditch.

Joskin—a rustic or countryman.

Killer or Keeler—large tub, used for brewing.
Keep-room—best room or parlour.
Key-beer—best beer, kept under lock and key.
Kitling—cat.
Kiender-sidows—kinder sideways.

Marndarin—w a n d e r i n g about, sauntering.
Mardle—small talk, gossip.
Mander—manner.
Mort—many.
Mud-skuppit—w o o d e n s h o v e l used for cleaning out ditches.
Mor, Mawther—young girl.
Morphadite—a waggon formed by joining two carts; the shafts of the hind one (a tumbril) are fastened to the shorter cart in front.
Middlestead—central bay of a barn.
Mingin-hutch, Mingin—to mix dough or pastry.
Mawkin—scarecrow.

Nunetimes—noontime, dinner.

Ongain—awkward, unsteady and unreliable.

Popples—poplars.
Plumpandikkalla'd—perpendicu-lar, straight down.
Pightle—a little field.
Pomp—pump.
Paigle—cowslip.
Pie-pan—dish.
Pin-o-throat—Adam's apple.
Plancher—board.
Pot-days—cooking days. It was the custom even amongst sub-stantial farmers to cook only three days a week, of which Sunday was one. These called pot-days.
Pitman—smallest pig in the litter.

Quackle—choke.

Rokey—misty, rainy, foggy.
Roved—congealed.

Spickets and Fansets—spigots.
Scuppit—a shovel.
Seggen, Segs—rushes.
Suzzles—a mixture of drinks.
Sueing—leaking.
Stroop—windpipe.
Swobble—spill over.
Sybbits—banns of marriage.

Seal o' the day—time of the day in salutation.

Trosshle—threshold.
Twizzling—turning.

Wittlepoke—victual or food bag.
Weeshoed—to the right.
Wash—a sunken sandy lane.
Wedge—kettle wedge, i.e. the piece of wood that makes the kettle boil.
Woosh—go to the right.

PORTWAY REPRINTS

EARLIER TITLES AVAILABLE FROM STOCK

Non-fiction

Braddock, Joseph	HAUNTED HOUSES
Cardus, Neville	DAYS IN THE SUN
Cobbett, William	COTTAGE ECONOMY
Day, J. Wentworth	GHOSTS AND WITCHES
Edmonds, Charles	A SUBALTERN'S WAR
Gandy, Ida	A WILTSHIRE CHILDHOOD
Gibbons, Floyd	RED KNIGHT OF GERMANY
Gibbs, P.	FROM BAPAUME TO PASSEHENDAELE
Grant, I. F.	ECONOMIC HISTORY OF SCOTLAND
Harris, John	RECOLLECTIONS OF RIFLEMAN HARRIS
Hitchcock, F. C.	STAND TO: A Diary of the Trenches
Jones, Jack	GIVE ME BACK MY HEART
Jones, Jack	UNFINISHED JOURNEY
Jones, Jack	ME AND MINE
Lowe, George	BECAUSE IT IS THERE
O'Mara, Pat	AUTOBIOGRAPHY OF A LIVERPOOL IRISH SLUMMY
D'Oyley, Elizabeth	JAMES, DUKE OF MONMOUTH
Price, Harry	THE MOST HAUNTED HOUSE IN ENGLAND
Price, Harry	THE END OF BORLEY RECTORY
Stamper, Joseph	LESS THAN THE DUST
Stoker, Bram	FAMOUS IMPOSTERS
Tangye, Derek	TIME WAS MINE
Tangye, Derek	WENT THE DAY WELL
Thompson, P. A.	LIONS LED BY DONKEYS
Vigilant	RICHTOFEN—Red Knight of the Air
Villiers, Alan	SONS OF SINDBAD
Von Richtofen	THE RED AIR FIGHTER

Fiction

Ainsworth, W. Harrison	GUY FAWKES
Anthony, Evelyn	CURSE NOT THE KING
Anthony, Evelyn	IMPERIAL HIGHNESS
Ashton, Helen	FOOTMAN IN POWDER
Barke, James	THE END OF HIGH BRIDGE
Barke, James	THE SONG IN THE GREEN THORN TREE
Barke, James	THE WELL OF THE SILENT HARP
Barke, James	THE WONDER OF ALL THE GAY WORLD
Barke, James	THE CREST OF THE BROKEN WAVE
Barke, James	THE WIND THAT SHAKES THE BARLEY
Benson, R. H.	LORD OF THE WORLD
Benson, R. H.	COME RACK, COME ROPE
Besant, Walter	DOROTHY FORSTER
Blain, William	WITCH'S BLOOD

Blaker, Richard	MEDAL WITHOUT BAR
Brophy, John	WATERFRONT
Brophy, John	GENTLEMAN OF STRATFORD
Broster, D. K.	SHIPS IN THE BAY
Broster, D. K.	SEA WITHOUT A HAVEN
Broster, D. K.	CHILD ROYAL
Broster, D. K. & Taylor, G. W.	CHANTERMERLE
Broster, D. K. & Taylor, G. W.	WORLD UNDER SNOW
Buck, Pearl	THE MOTHER
Buck, Pearl	THE PROUD HEART
Burney, Fanny	CAMILLA—in 5 volumes
Caldwell, Taylor	THE EAGLES GATHER
Caldwell, Taylor	TENDER VICTORY
Caldwell, Taylor	THE BEAUTIFUL IS VANISHED
Cloete, Stuart	THE CURVE AND THE TUSK
Collins, Wilkie	ARMADALE
Cookson, Catherine	COLOUR BLIND
Cookson, Catherine	FIFTEEN STREETS
Cookson, Catherine	KATE HANNIGAN
Cookson, Catherine	FANNY McBRIDE
Cookson, Catherine	MAGGIE ROWAN
Cookson, Catherine	ROONEY
Cordell, A.	RAPE OF THE FAIR COUNTRY
Corke, Helen	NEUTRAL GROUND
Crockett, S. R.	THE GREY MAN
Croker, B. M.	THE YOUNGEST MISS MOWBRAY
Cusack, Dymphna	COME IN SPINNER
& James, Florence	
Darlington, W. A.	ALF'S BUTTON
Davies, Rhys	THE TRIP TO LONDON
Davies, Rhys	THE BLACK VENUS
Dumas, Alexandre	THE LADY OF THE CAMELLIAS
Dumas, Alexandre	THE CORSICAN BROTHERS
Eca de Queiroz, Jose	COUSIN BASILIO
Eyles, Margaret	MARGARET PROTESTS
Ferber, Edna	GIANT
Ferrier, Susan	THE INHERITANCE
Field, Rachel	AND NOW TOMORROW
Firbank, T.	BRIDE TO THE MOUNTAIN
Godden, R.	BLACK NARCISSUS
Golding, Louis	MAGNOLIA STREET
Golding, Louis	CAMBERWELL BEAUTY
Golding, Louis	THE LOVING BROTHERS
Greenwood, Walter	HIS WORSHIP THE MAYOR
Gunn, Neil	BUTCHER'S BROOM
Gunn, Neil	THE GREY COAST
Gunn, Neil	THE KEY OF THE CHEST
Household, Geoffrey	THE THIRD HOUR
James, Henry	WHAT MASIE KNEW
Jenkins, Robin	HAPPY FOR THE CHILD
Jones, Jack	RIVER OUT OF EDEN
Jones, Jack	BLACK PARADE
Jones, Jack	BIDDEN TO THE FEAST
Jones, Jack	RHONDDA ROUNDABOUT
Jones, Jack	LUCKY LEAR
Jones, Jack	SOME TRUST IN CHARIOTS
Jones, Jack	OFF TO PHILADELPHIA
	IN THE MORNING

Oliver, Jane	IN NO STRANGE LAND
Oliver, Jane	THE LION IS COME
Oliver, Jane	CROWN FOR A PRISONER
Oliver, Jane	SUNSET AT NOON
Oliver, Jane	SING MORNING STAR
Ouida	UNDER TWO FLAGS
Ouida	MOTHS
Pargeter, Edith	THE EIGHTH CHAMPION OF CHRISTENDOM
Pargeter, Edith	RELUCTANT ODYSSEY
Pargeter, Edith	WARFARE ACCOMPLISHED
Pargeter, Edith	MOST LOVING MORE FOLLY
Pargeter, Edith	ORDINARY PEOPLE
Pargeter, Edith	THE HEAVEN TREE
Pargeter, Edith	THE GREEN BRANCH
Pargeter, Edith	THE SCARLET SEED
Phillpotts, Eden	THE RIVER
Phillpotts, Eden	CHILDREN OF THE MIST
Phillpotts, Eden	THE MOTHER
Phillpotts, Eden	THE HUMAN BOY
Phillpotts, Eden	THE HUMAN BOY AGAIN
Phillpotts, Eden	THE FOREST ON THE HILL
Raymond, Ernest	THE KILBURN TALE
Raymond, Ernest	CHILD OF NORMAN'S END
Raymond, Ernest	DAPHNE BRUNO
Raymond, Ernest	THE FULFILMENT OF DAPHNE BRUNO
Raymond, Ernest	A SONG OF THE TIDE
Raymond, Ernest	A FAMILY THAT WAS
Riley, William	JERRY AND BEN
Riley, William	LAYCOCK OF LONEDALE
Shellabarger, Samuel	CAPTAIN FROM CASTLE
Shiel, M. P.	THE LAST MIRACLE
Shiel, M. P.	PRINCE ZALESKI
Sienkiewicz, Henryk	THE DELUGE—two volumes
Sienkiewicz, Henryk	PAN MICHAEL
Smith, Betty	A TREE GROWS IN BROOKLYN
Soubiran, André	THE DOCTORS
Sutton, Graham	NORTH STAR
Sutton, Graham	THE ROWAN TREE
Tilsley, Frank	CHAMPION ROAD
Timms, E. V.	HILLS OF HATE
Timms, E. V.	FAR CARAVAN
Tunstall, Beatrice	SHINY NIGHT
Turnbull, Agnes Sligh	THE DAY MUST DAWN
Turnbull, Agnes Sligh	THE ROLLING YEARS
Turnbull, Agnes Sligh	REMEMBER THE END
Vaughan, Hilda	HARVEST HOME
Walpole, H.	FORTITUDE
Walpole, H.	KATHERINE CHRISTIAN
Warren, R. P.	A HEAVEN'S GATE
Wells, H. G.	MR. BLETTSWORTHY ON RAMPOLE ISLAND
Wells, H. G.	THE SHAPE OF THINGS TO COME
Wilkins, Vaughan	SEVEN TEMPEST
Wilkins, Vaughan	A KING RELUCTANT
Wilkins, Vaughan	CITY OF FROZEN FIRE
Young, Francis Brett	DR. BRADLEY REMEMBERS